PREHISTORY AND CLASSICAL PERIOD

Edited by Tim Cooke

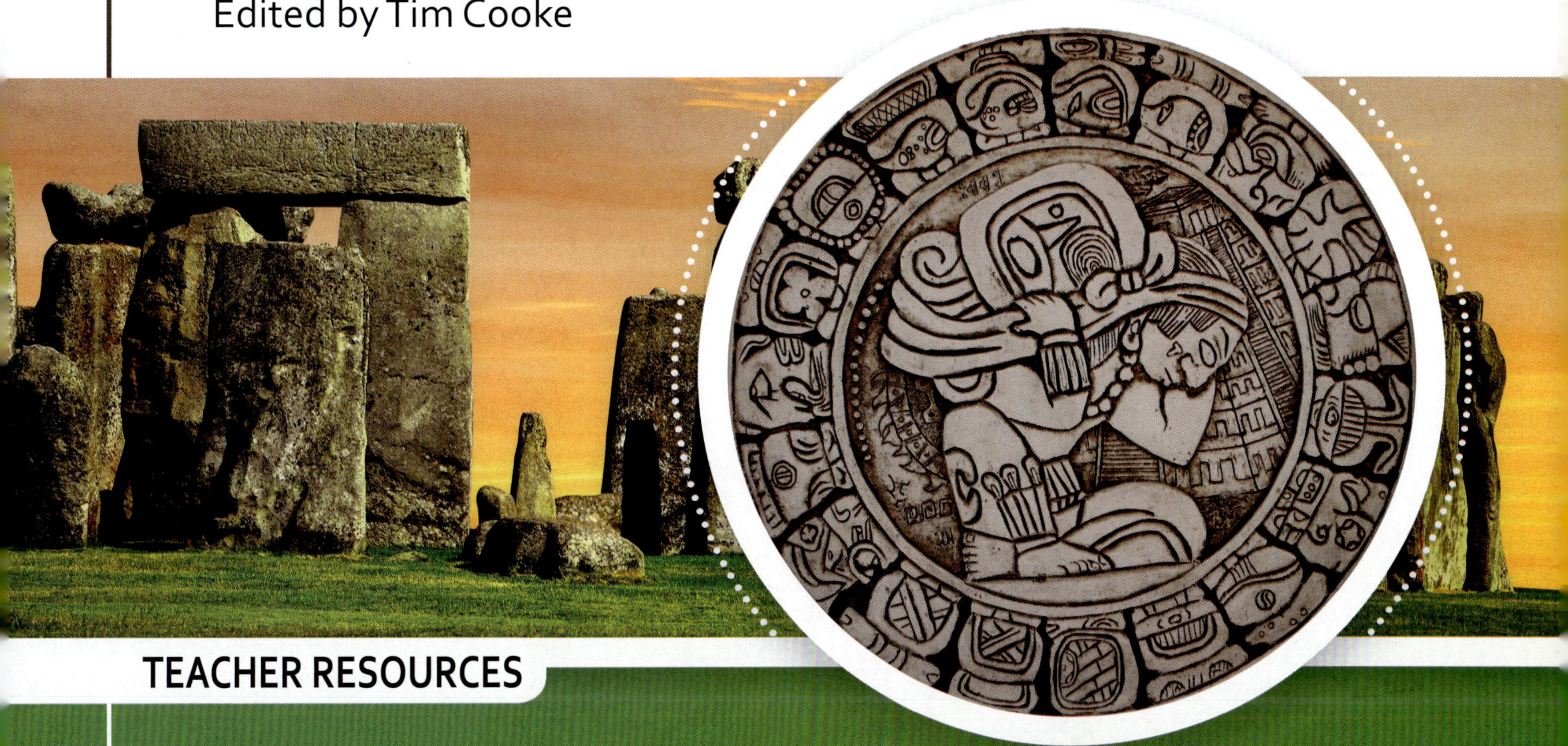

TEACHER RESOURCES

SCIENTIFIC DISCOVERY

LIGHTBOX
openlightbox.com

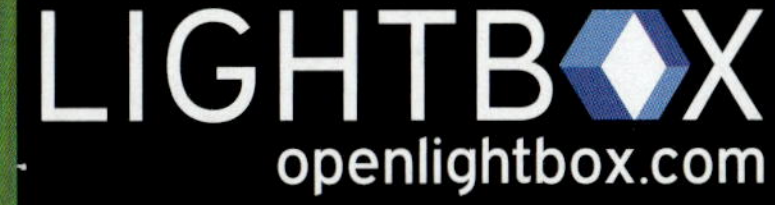

LIGHTBOX

Go to
www.openlightbox.com
and enter this book's
unique code.

ACCESS CODE

LBXU3348

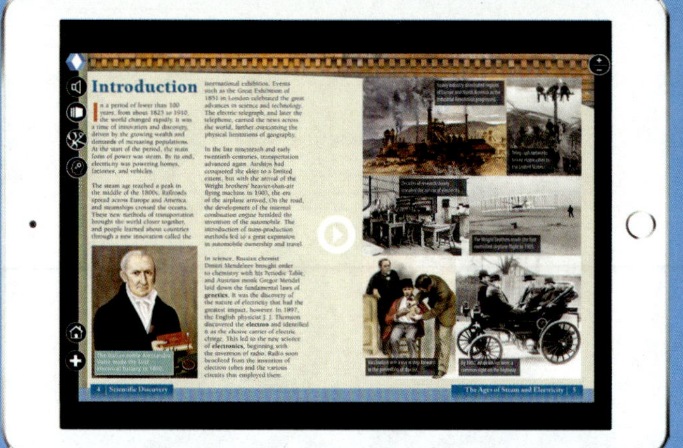

Lightbox is an all-inclusive digital solution for the teaching and learning of curriculum topics in an original, groundbreaking way. Lightbox is based on National Curriculum Standards.

STANDARD FEATURES OF LIGHTBOX

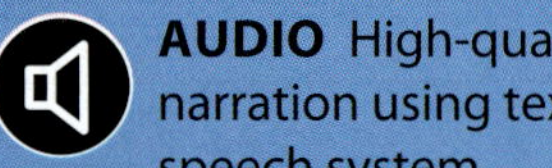

AUDIO High-quality narration using text-to-speech system

VIDEOS Embedded high-definition video clips

ACTIVITIES Printable PDFs that can be emailed and graded

WEBLINKS Curated links to external, child-safe resources

SLIDESHOWS Pictorial overviews of key concepts

TRANSPARENCIES Step-by-step layering of maps, diagrams, charts, and timelines

INTERACTIVE MAPS Interactive maps and aerial satellite imagery

QUIZZES Ten multiple choice questions that are automatically graded and emailed for teacher assessment

KEY WORDS Matching key concepts to their definitions

MORE Extra information and details on the subject

FIRST HAND Letters, diaries, and other primary sources

DOCS Speeches, newspaper articles, and other historical documents

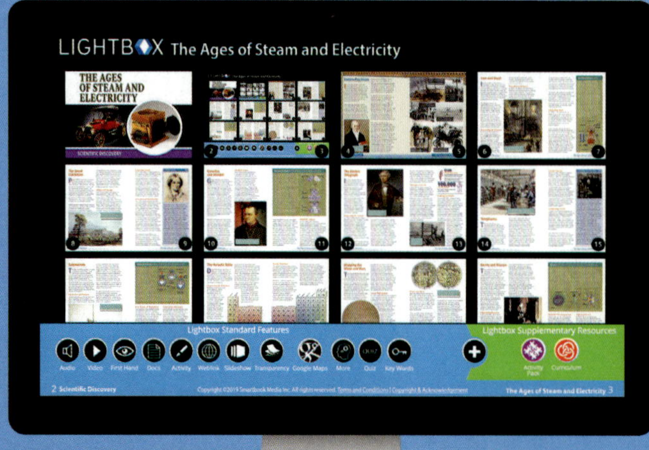

Contents

Introduction

The history of science is as long as the history of humankind itself. Early people shaped stone pebbles into tools. They used the tools to help them fashion weapons and other **artifacts** from bone, antler, and wood. They also learned how to use fire. Fire was used for cooking and heating, and as a source of light.

The next major advance came when people learned how to cultivate plants for food, particularly cereals. This marked the beginning of farming. Rather than roaming around to look for food, people began to live in permanent settlements. They also began to use animals for food, wool, hides, and to pull or carry loads.

In the third century BC, Archimedes designed a range of new machines and weapons.

The spread of agriculture enabled farmers to produce enough food to allow more people to move off the land and settle in towns and cities.

Recorded history began with the invention of forms of writing. This development meant that information could be shared and passed on from one generation to another. Early peoples also developed numbers and counting systems, together with standard weights and measures. This allowed accurate records to be made of crops harvested and traded. To keep track of the seasons so farmers would know when to sow and harvest their crops, people devised calendars. With the calendar came a growing understanding of the night sky. This marked the beginnings of astronomy, the first of the sciences to be studied.

With developing civilizations came new construction technologies. The Egyptians and **Mesoamericans** built vast **pyramids**, while the ancient Greeks built temples and the Romans are renowned for their roads and aqueducts, some of which are still in use. Major conflicts between societies also increased, however. The development of ever more sophisticated weapons of war became an essential part of technological innovation and scientific research. Toward the end of the period, it is possible to identify the first true scientists and philosophers, such as the Greek mathematician, engineer, and inventor Archimedes.

As agriculture improved from about 11,000 BC, farmers grew enough food to enable populations to grow.

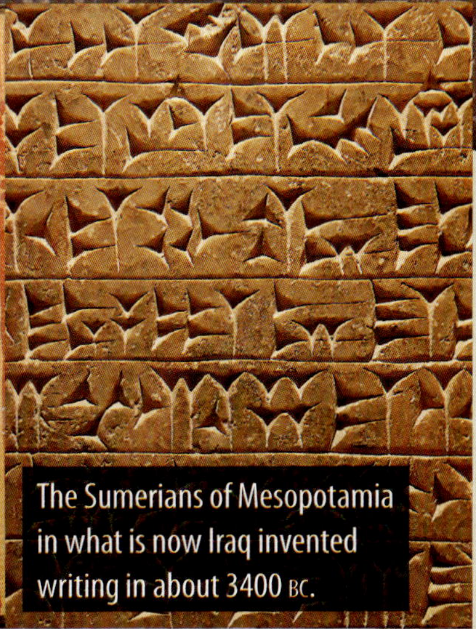

The Sumerians of Mesopotamia in what is now Iraq invented writing in about 3400 BC.

Ancient astronomers studied the moon to track the passage of the seasons.

From the 300s BC, waterwheels harnessed the power of water to turn millstones for grinding grain.

From 5000 BC, metalworkers learned to produce stronger tools and weapons.

Ancient peoples on both sides of the Atlantic built gigantic pyramids as part of their religious practices.

ACTIVITIES

Video

Period 1 in World History

Watch the video to learn more about prehistory and the classical period.

1. Where did the Neolithic revolution start? Describe the five things that characterized this period. Explain the discovery that led to this revolution.
2. Describe how people got to America. How long ago did this occur? Explain why they could not take the same route today.
3. List the five early civilizations mentioned in the video in chronological order. Analyze which of these civilizations had the most influence on early human history. Support your answer with evidence. Are there other civilizations that were important during this time?

Weblink

Ancient History Encyclopedia: Science

Read the article to learn more about the main scientific achievements of early civilizations.

1. Describe what Carl Sagan says is necessary for the impetus for science. Do you agree with the statement that if people "lived on a planet where nothing ever changed, there would be little to do?" Say why or why not.
2. What did the Cherokee of North America think caused eclipses? What did the Vikings think was happening during eclipses? Describe how people came to realize that eclipses occurred in a regular, repeating pattern.
3. Describe the numeral system the Babylonians used. Explain in what way or ways this system is still used today. How accurate was the Babylonian calculation of pi?

RUBRIC

Write an Abstract

Students will use their library or Google Scholar to find a scientific research article or study related to the use of tools in early humans, then write a 300-word abstract. An exemplary abstract will meet the following criteria:

- States the research question or problem that the author is answering
- Indicates the significance of the issue
- Describes and explains methods used by the scientist(s)
- Explains why the methods used by the scientist(s) were appropriate
- Explains why this article or study stands out and how it is different from others
- Clearly states how the article or study advances knowledge about the topic, why it is important, and how it can be used
- Introductory statement is clear, concise, and engaging
- Purpose is clear, concise, and relevant
- Explanation of the findings includes what was expected, discovered, accomplished, collected, and produced
- Clearly states the conclusion
- Conclusion describes how the work contributes to the field
- Writing is appropriate and free from grammatical errors

Early Humans

Human ancestors were making tools about 2.3 million years ago in Ethiopia and about 2.25 million years ago in China. Nearly 2 million years ago at Olduvai Gorge, Tanzania, "handy man" (*Homo habilis*) made choppers by striking one stone against another to form a sharpened edge. Choppers were used for cutting or sawing, and the blunt end of the stone would smash stone or bone. *Homo habilis* left so many choppers of different sizes and types that their output is known as the Oldowan Industry.

Homo habilis lived only in Africa. A later species, *Homo erectus*, migrated out of Africa and spread across Eurasia. *Homo erectus* lived from 1.85 million years ago until about 400,000 years ago and made more sophisticated tools than those of earlier species. The earliest tools associated with *Homo erectus* were found in Olduvai Gorge and are about 1.4 million years old. They are called the Acheulean Industry.

The Hammer

Instead of striking identical stones together, Acheulean toolmakers used stone hammers to make cleavers and hand axes, with straighter cutting edges than the old choppers. By about 1 million years ago, they had discovered how to use hammers made from deer antlers. This development allowed them to work with greater precision to make a much wider range of tools for cutting, drilling, shaping, and hammering.

Neanderthals (*Homo sapiens neanderthalensis*) lived in Europe, the Mediterranean, and parts of the Middle East at the same time as modern humans. They first appeared about 100,000 years ago, and they became **extinct** about 30,000 years ago. Neanderthals made a variety of stone tools.

Many remains of early human ancestors have been found in Olduvai Gorge in Tanzania.

Modern humans, *Homo sapiens*, were making much more efficient tools by around 40,000 years ago. In France, they produced up to 80 different kinds of stone implements. People were also making tools with stone blades fixed to bone or antler handles. Cro-Magnon people, who lived in southern Europe from 35,000 to 10,000 years ago, made chisels, awls, and blades for scraping animal skins to make leather. In parts of southwestern France between 21,000 and 17,000 years ago, workers were producing blades shaped like willow and laurel leaves.

Archaeological Remains

Evidence of ancient technology comes from **archaeological** remains such as stone tools. Many artifacts made from wood and plant fibers have rotted away, but a few examples have survived. They show that arrowheads and spearheads had wooden shafts, and that the first clothing may have been a skirt made from cords hung from a belt. People were likely twisting fibers into cords by 20,000 years ago. They wove willow stalks to make baskets and fish traps and used cords to make fishing nets. They may have made cloth in the same way. By about 2700 BC, silk was being woven into cloth in China.

Boatbuilders

A **rock carving** from northern Europe, made between 9,000 and 10,000 years ago, shows what appears to be a boat carrying hunters or fishers. The boat seems to have a frame, in which case it may have resembled the traditional kayak still used by the Inuit, with a strong wooden frame covered in animal skin. Where they could find big enough trees, people hollowed out tree trunks to make dugout canoes. The earliest boat of this type in Europe was found at Pesse in the Netherlands. It is made from pine and is approximately 8,000 years old. People also split wood into planks to build boats. Boats built from planks found in eastern England have been dated at 2,900 years old.

Making Fire

The fire drill was probably one of the earliest human inventions. It uses a wooden bow to rotate a blunt-ended fire stick in a hollow in a piece of softer dry wood. The stick spins first one way and then the other as the bow is pulled back and forth, heating the end of the stick.

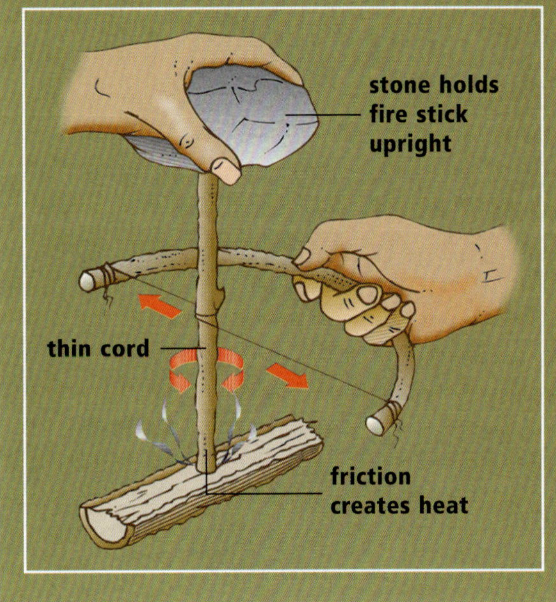

ACTIVITIES

Transparency

Making Fire

Examine the diagram and research online to learn more about early methods of making fire.

1. What is the name of the device used to make fire? Describe how it works. What creates the heat?
2. Where has evidence of use of this device been found? Describe three other similar devices that use friction to create heat.

Weblink

Human Ancestors May Have Used Tools Half-Million Years Earlier Than Thought

Review the article to learn more about recent research into early humans' use of tools.

1. Describe what the study analyzed. What are the two hand postures that are said to be important for tool use? Explain why they are important.
2. Analyze why experts view the timing of the first tools as significant in human history. What has been cited as evidence to suggest tool use in Ethiopia 3.4 million years ago? Explain what might be the reason why this evidence has not been universally accepted.
3. Describe what is said to put the biggest demands on the precision grip. Do you agree that examining the internal structure of hand bones is a better method of determining early tool use than looking at the external shape of hand bones? Support your answer with evidence. In what way does this study lead the way forward in the investigation of early humans' use of tools?

Origin of Crops

There are more than 75,000 species of edible plants in the world, but 60 percent of the world's food comes from just three plants. These are wheat, corn, and rice. They became important as early humans began domesticating wild crops. The first attempts to domesticate cereal grains came in the Middle East about 10,000 to 11,000 years ago. In other parts of the world, different peoples domesticated the plants that occurred naturally. This led to a wide variety of crops being produced.

KOSTER, ILLINOIS
For much of the prehistoric period, American societies were hunter-gatherers. In northeastern regions, peoples domesticated gourds, squashes, and sunflowers, for their seeds. In southern North America and Central America, at sites such as Koster, crops included corn, beans, squashes, tomatoes, sweet potato, papayas, and avocados.

LEGEND

- Water
- Land
- Major agricultural region

Approximate date farming began

- about 8000 BC
- about 6500 BC
- about 6700 BC
- about 0 BC
- about 3000 BC

N

0 2,000 miles
0 4,000 kilometers

CARAL, PERU
In lowland regions of South America, such as the ancient coastal city of Caral, people grew manioc, peanuts, pineapple, beans, squashes, sweet potatoes, papayas, and cocoa. In the Andes Mountains, farmers grew potatoes, chili peppers, gourds, and quinoa.

ARCTIC OCEAN

SUBEIXI, XINJIANG, CHINA

Early Chinese agriculture in settlements such as Subeixi was based on rice. It also featured millet, soybeans, buckwheat, tea, aduki beans, peaches, oranges, and apricots.

ASIA

EUROPE

AFRICA

INDIAN OCEAN

SOUTH ATLANTIC OCEAN

AUSTRALIA

ÇATALHÖYÜK, TURKEY

Agriculture originated in the Middle East in about 10,000 BC. By 7500 BC, farming had spread to Turkey, where it supported a large city at Çatalhöyük. The earliest domesticated plants included barley, flax, lentils, wheat, peas, chickpeas, carrots, date palms, lemons, lettuce, and beets.

TILEMSI VALLEY, MALI

West African peoples began farming before 1 BC in fertile regions such as the Tilemsi Valley in what is now Mali. They grew pearl millet and cow pea, together with African rice, watermelons, yams, and okra.

ACTIVITIES

Google Maps

Origin of Crops

Examine the map of the origin of crops.

1. Analyze why the major agricultural regions developed in these locations. Give reasons for your answer.
2. Research online the location of the biggest producers of wheat, corn, and rice today. Explain why production of these food crops might be in those locations.

Weblink

Early Agriculture and Development

Read the link on agriculture and development.

1. Explain why early human populations migrated with the seasons. Describe why the food supply of these hunter-gatherers was relatively stable.
2. When and where did the agricultural revolution develop? Describe some of the theories that have been put forward about why agriculture arose. Evaluate which of these theories seems the most plausible. Give reasons for your answer.
3. Describe the five ways in which human society changed as a result of crop domestication. Explain what problems developed due to agriculture. Which, if any, of these is still problematic for human societies today?

RUBRIC

Analyzing a Scientific Video

Students will watch and assess a video related to a scientific discovery, and write an analysis of the video. An exemplary video analysis will meet the following criteria.

- Identifies the purpose of the video
- Identifies the intended audience of the video
- Identifies the video as a primary or secondary source
- Discusses the scientific and social context of the video
- Describes how the content of the video is presented
- Summarizes the information and opinions presented in the video
- Analyzes the quality of the content presented in the video
- Assesses the effectiveness of the video
- Determines whether the images and graphics used in the video relate to the content
- Determines whether the video is easy to follow and understand
- Gives the analysis a clear and consistent purpose
- Organizes the analysis in a logical, effective manner
- Presents a strong, clear argument about the video
- Provides strong and accurate details to support the argument about the video
- Considers other perspectives on the purpose and effectiveness of the video
- Cites all sources used in the analysis

Development of the Wheel

Six thousand years ago, humans used drag technology to move loads. Drag devices included plows, sledges, and travois, which are made up of two trailing poles for dragging loads. In some parts of the world, objects such as rocks and boats were moved using log rollers. As the object moved forward, rollers were taken from behind and replaced in front. These rollers may have been the starting point for the invention of the cartwheel.

At some point, it seems likely that someone combined the use of a sledge with the rolling logs. After a set of logs had been used for some time, they would become worn where they scraped against the sledge. Eventually, the sledge would settle into the worn section of the rollers. This may have given people the idea of the axle wheel. An axle has a small circumference, so it takes less energy to turn than a whole wheel. A relatively small amount of energy spent turning an axle is magnified into the turning of a large wheel.

There are problems with the roller theory of the invention of the wheel. Whole logs split and fall apart quite easily when rolled under pressure. Tall, straight trees were not abundant in the Middle East, where the first evidence for transport wheels appears.

The development of a wheel constructed to rotate on a fixed axle is used by archaeologists as an indicator of a relatively advanced civilization. The earliest evidence of wheels that turned on an axle dates to about 3200 BC. Sumerian artists produced many pictures of carts with solid wheels. The wheels were apparently made from two pieces of plank that were bracketed together and cut into a circular shape. The axles went through the center of each wheel and were fixed in place by lynchpins.

Pottery wheels rotate at a steady speed. This helps the potter create an evenly-shaped pot.

The Aztec did not use wheels for transportation, but made toylike wheeled artifacts.

Working Wheels

The first wheels were probably not intended for transportation. Evidence from about 3500 BC shows that potters used simple turntables to help them create evenly shaped pots. These potters' wheels were developed by the Greeks and Egyptians into **flywheels** that could convert pulses of energy, such as the pressing of a treadle, or foot pedal, into smooth, continuous motion. The flywheel was to become as important as the vehicular wheel. The Greeks also came up with other variations on the wheel. The fourth and third centuries BC saw the development of cogs, gearwheels, and pulleys. The waterwheel was another important variation on the basic axled design.

Since ancient times, there have been several more wheel innovations. The Chinese began using spinning wheels for manufacturing yarn between 500 and 1000 AD. The same development reached Europe several hundred years later, early in the thirteenth century. As the spinning wheel turns, it rotates a spindle that twists plant fibers together to make thread much faster than can be done by hand. In the Americas, meanwhile, peoples such as the Aztec and Inca understood the wheel but did not make wheeled vehicles. It may be that they believed the wheel was sacred, and reserved for the use of the gods.

Wheels of War

Wheels appeared on war chariots built by the Sumerians in about 2500 BC. Such vehicles could give armies an advantage in battle, but they would have been very heavy and difficult to control. About 500 years later, the Sumerians developed spoked wheels, which made chariots much lighter and more maneuverable. Over the next 500 years, the design of the wheel spread and was refined by other peoples, including the Egyptians and the Romans.

Different civilizations may have come up with the wheel at different times. In China, for example, the wheel appeared in about 2800 BC. The Chinese also appear to have been the first to develop the wheelbarrow, in about 100 AD. It was several centuries before European technology caught up. A thirteenth-century stained-glass window in Chartres Cathedral in northern France shows the earliest depiction of a wheelbarrow in the Western world.

ACTIVITIES

Video

Hidden Histories: The Wheel
Watch the video to learn more about the history of the wheel.

1. When is some of the earliest evidence for the wheel dated to? What evidence for the use of the wheel have archaeologists found at the ancient city of Ur? What is the date for the oldest reliably dated wheel?
2. What invention from 2000 BC was a key point in the history of the wheel? Describe the type of vehicle that developed from this invention. What is said to be the main appeal of this vehicle?
3. When did chariots first appear in China? What contribution related to the wheel did the Romans make? Explain why wheels seem to have been used only on models or toys in the Americas.

Weblink

A Salute to the Wheel
Examine the article to learn some little-known facts about the wheel.

1. What distinguishes the wheel from most other inventions? What does evidence indicate was the first use of wheels? What date is given for the first use of wheels?
2. The wheel of fortune is referred to in classical works of literature by Cicero, Pindar, Geoffrey Chaucer, and William Shakespeare. What other works of literature would refer to the wheel of fortune? Investigate how the Western concept of the wheel of fortune has parallels in Eastern civilizations.
3. Describe the oldest design for a perpetual motion device. What are the two laws of thermodynamics the design violates?

The Egyptians used oxen to plow the fields, making it easier for them to plant and grow grain.

Domestication of Animals

The domestication of livestock probably began around 8000 BC, when goats and mouflon, or sheep, were taken into captivity in East Asia and Mesopotamia. They were followed in about 7000 BC by wild pigs. Young animals would have been caught and kept captive until they grew to a useful size. Keeping fully grown animals alive meant their meat would stay fresh for later use.

By about 6500 BC, cattle were kept under domestication in Africa and India. Chickens were domesticated in Southeast Asia in about 5500 BC. Other uses for captive animals followed, such as sources of milk, blood, and wool. There is evidence that, by about 4000 BC, people in the Middle East were harnessing the strength of animals to drag heavy loads or pull plows. At the same time in Europe, horses began to be kept. To begin with they would have provided just meat and milk, but within a relatively short time people were riding them. By 2000 BC, horses were animals of status, ridden by important people. They were used in war to intimidate the enemy, ridden by cavalry or pulling chariots. Bactrian camels were domesticated in Afghanistan by about 2500 BC. In the New World, the llama was domesticated in about 3000 BC, and the guinea pig, or cavy, in 2000 BC. The guinea pig was bred for meat long before it became a popular pet.

Choosing an Animal

Some animals are better suited to domestication than others. The cheapest and easiest animals to keep are grazers, such as cattle and sheep. They can be turned out to forage for themselves. Goats and camels are equally easy, but need more watching because they will eat nearly anything. Horses, on the other hand, need to be provided with grain as well as grass. This makes them more expensive to keep and explains why they were domesticated later than other livestock. Another economic consideration is the speed at which an animal grows and matures. From a farmer's perspective, only animals that reach a useful size and reproductive maturity quickly are worth keeping.

Other factors that determine domestication relate to an animal's behavior. Temperament is important. Cattle and horses are far more easily handled than zebras and hippos, for example, and sheep and pigs are less panicky than deer and antelope.

The two-humped Bactrian camel is capable of carrying heavy loads or people.

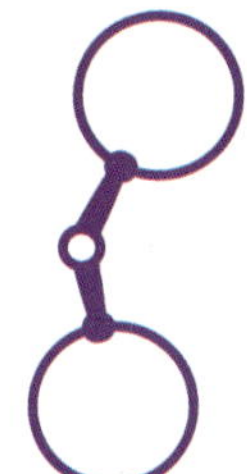

6,000
YEARS OLD
The age of bridle bits found in Ukraine. The bits show that people were riding horses by this time.

1627 AD
EXTINCTION
The date the last wild aurochs, the ancestor of domestic cattle, became extinct.

Animals that are stressed in captivity tend not to breed well. Another characteristic shared by successfully domesticated animals is the tendency to form social groups. The wild ancestors of domesticated animals, such as dogs, all live in hierarchical groups. They are used to having a leader, and so it was relatively easy for them to submit to human dominance.

In many cases, the wild species from which domestic animals have evolved are extinct. Today, there are no pure-bred wild horses, dromedary camels, llamas, or guinea pigs, only those descended from escaped domestics. Wild Bactrian camels and wild yak are highly endangered. There was probably never a wild alpaca. This cousin of the llama may have evolved as a domesticated animal, perhaps as the result of hybridization between llamas and wild vicuna.

ACTIVITIES

Weblink

Our Furry Friends: the History of Animal Domestication
Review the link to learn more about the history of the domestication of animals.

1. What animal was probably the first to be domesticated? What evidence have scientists found to support that theory? Which animal played a large role in Egyptian civilization?
2. List the first animals to be domesticated for food use. What evidence do scientists use to determine when milk-bearing animals were domesticated? Summarize the ways in which the domestication of animals helped civilizations to emerge.
3. Where and when was the first conclusive evidence of horse riding? Explain why the riding of horses was a significant development.
4. List the six criteria that an animal must meet in order to domesticate it. Are there any other criteria that may be important? Give reasons for your answer.

RUBRIC

Create a Scientific Poster

Students will create a scientific poster exploring the topic of writing and numbers. An exemplary poster will meet the following criteria:

- The poster has a title that suggests the chosen topic or theme
- The poster presents relevant and accurate information about the topic or theme
- The format of the poster is appropriate to the content, purpose, and audience for which it was designed
- Visuals such as pictures, photographs, charts, tables, scientific drawings, or diagrams add to the effectiveness of the poster
- The poster is well organized and the poster elements work well together
- The use of appropriate graphic design tools, space, color, texture, and shape effectively creates an aesthetically pleasing product
- The poster draws attention
- Language chosen for the poster is accurate, informative, and concise

Writing and Numbers

Writing developed as a way of keeping records to help organize society and trade. At first, people drew pictures of things. These drawings then became simpler in form. "Sun" might be a small circle inside a larger circle, and water might be a wavy line. Signs could be drawn quickly and remained recognizable even when they were small. In time, they came to have more than one meaning. The sign for "Sun" also meant "day," or in Egypt the Sun-god Re (or Ra). Over time, signs came to represent sounds as well as objects, or simply sounds. Writing in which pictures represent sounds is called "hieroglyphic," and the best-known type appeared in Egypt around 3100 BC. By about 2700 BC, Egyptian hieroglyphic writing had been more or less standardized. It remained in use for some 3,000 years.

Cuneiform Writing

Another system of writing emerged in Mesopotamia. While it also began as a system of stylized pictures, it developed differently from Egyptian hieroglyphics. Whereas Egyptian scribes wrote on **papyrus**, the scribes in Mesopotamian pressed a writing tool called a stylus into a tablet of soft clay, making a wedge or round shape. This type of writing is called cuneiform. It came into use in about 2400 BC. Cuneiform was used by the Sumerians, the Assyrians, and the Babylonians. It also spread to Persia. Cuneiform remained in use for nearly 2,000 years.

Most modern letters can be traced back to the Proto Canaanite and Phoenician alphabets.

Proto Canaanite	Early letter names and meanings	Phoenician	Early Greek	Early monumental Latin	Modern English
	alp oxhead				A
	bêt house				B
	gaml throwstick				C
	digg fish				D
	hô(?) man calling				E
	wô mace				F
	zê(n) ?				
	hê(t) fence?				H
	tê(t) spindle?				
	yad arm				I
	kapp palm				K
	lamd ox-goad				L
	mêm water				M
	nahs snake				N
	cên eye				O
	pi't corner?				P
	sa(d) plant				
	qu(p) ?				Q
	ra's head of man				R
	taan composite bow				S
	tô owner's mark				T

Alphabets

The first real alphabet is called the Proto Canaanite. It emerged in the Middle East in about 1700 BC. It used 30 symbols to represent sounds. From this, the Phoenician alphabet of 22 letters developed by about 1000 BC. It gave rise to Arabic, Hebrew, Latin, and Greek scripts. Chinese writing also developed from pictures. The pictures were inscribed on bones and shells that were thrown into the air. People believed the pattern in which they fell carried messages from the gods or from dead ancestors. These symbols were used from about 1700 BC. Over 1,500 years, they became more abstract.

Keeping Count

Record keepers also needed a way to write numbers. A picture can represent a cow, but it is not practical to represent 60 cows by drawing each one. In about 30,000 BC in what is now the Czech Republic, someone carved 55 notches in 11 groups of five on a wolf bone. The notches may refer to how many animals were killed in a hunt, although no one really knows. A stick or bone used in this way is called a tally stick.

Numerals for quantities greater than 10 were used in ancient Egypt in about 3400 BC, Mesopotamia in about 3000 BC, and in Crete by 1200 BC. Using 10 as a base was an obvious choice because humans have 10 fingers. The Babylonians and Sumerians were the major exceptions. They calculated to base 60.

The Epic of Gilgamesh

The Sumerians used cuneiform to keep records, but they also used it to write down stories and poems. In the *Epic of Gilgamesh*, Gilgamesh is a semidivine being of huge strength who builds walls to protect the city of Uruk. After the death of his friend Enkidu, Gilgamesh makes a dangerous journey to visit an immortal being named Upnapishtim, who had survived the Great Flood that destroyed all life on Earth. Gilgamesh wants to learn the secret of eternal life, but Upnapishtim explains that humans must accept that they are fated to die. The story was first written down around 2100 BC and repeated in different versions over about 2,000 years. The best-known version was written between 1300 and 1000 BC on 12 cuneiform tablets. They were discovered in 1853 in the library of King Ashubanipal in the city of Nineveh. Today, most historians believe that Gilgamesh may have been based on a real Mesopotamian king.

ACTIVITIES

Document

The Epic of Gilgamesh: Literature Review

Read the article about the epic of Gilgamesh.

1. Which Indian and Greek epics does the writer say the epic of Gilgamesh predates? Describe the literary convention that is used at the start of the epic. What is the effect of this convention?
2. Write a character portrait of Gilgamesh based on the descriptions in the article. Imagine you are describing him to a friend. Include both the strengths and weaknesses of his character, and his motivations. What effect does Gilgamesh's connection to Enkidu have on Gilgamesh?

Weblink

The Alphabet's Brilliant Conquest

Examine the article about the alphabet.

1. Describe the difference between writing and the alphabet. What was the main drawback of cuneiform and Egyptian hieroglyphic writing systems? Appraise the analogy the writer uses to draw the distinction between writing and the alphabet. Is it useful? Say why or why not.
2. What is the earliest-known example of an alphabet? Who do scholars think created this script? Explain in your own words what was revolutionary about this script. Describe two letters that are said to be based on hieroglyphics.

Ancient Medicine

Some of the earliest evidence for the existence of medicine as a science comes from Babylon. In the early 1700s BC, Babylonian law included penalties for doctors who made mistakes when treating their patients. If a doctor opened an abscess and the patient died, for example, the doctor's hands were cut off. As well as consulting doctors, Babylonians also left sick people lying in the street so that passersby could offer advice.

At that time, no one understood how the body functions. People believed there were two classes of illness. Trivial complaints, such as an upset stomach, headache, or cold, were part of everyday life. Ancient peoples such as the Babylonians and ancient Egyptians treated such conditions with whatever remedy seemed to work. They believed that more serious illnesses, such as fevers, smallpox, or dysentery, were caused by demons that had entered the body, or by angry gods. Treatment involved removing the worm or demon that was causing the symptoms or encouraging the soul to return to its proper place in the body. Practitioners used suction or physical manipulation of the patient's body to remove the cause of the disease as well as administering **herbal medicines** and performing incantations. Treatment often involved magic or religious ritual, and those who performed it were known as "medicine men" or "medicine women."

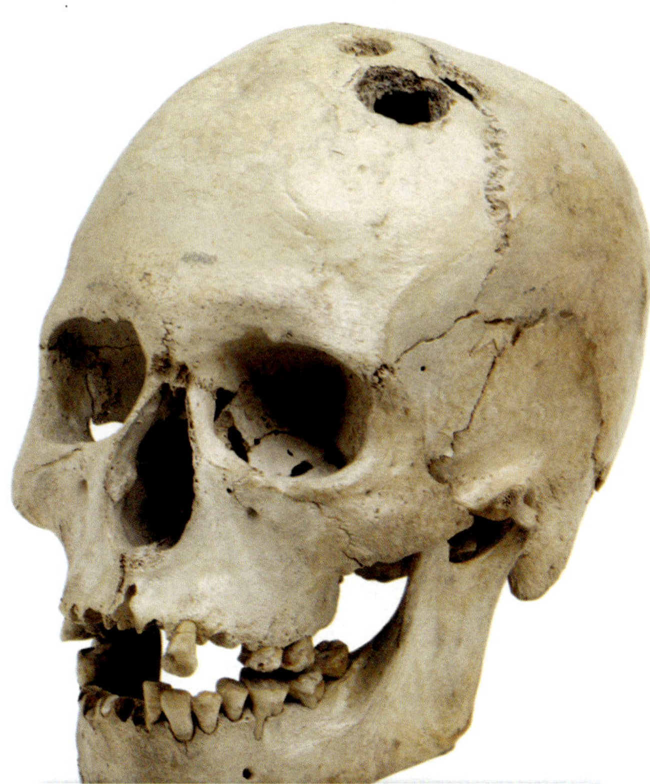

Prehistoric peoples believed that a hole drilled in the skull would relieve severe headaches and other maladies.

Drilling a small hole in the top of the skull was one way to allow whatever caused an illness to escape. This trepanning, was widely practiced. Prehistoric trepanned skulls have been found in Europe and South America. Bone has regrown around the holes, so the patients obviously survived.

People who carried out such surgery were highly respected. The Egyptian physician Imhotep, for example, was a government official, as well as being **astrologer** and architect to King Djoser, who reigned from 2630 to 2611 BC. Within 100 years of his death, Imhotep became the Egyptian god of medicine.

Medicine in Asia

Chinese medicine began more than 4,500 years ago. Chinese doctors believed that illness was caused by imbalances between the female and male cosmic principles, or yin and yang. Their treatment aimed to correct the imbalance. Doctors used herbal remedies, such as *Ephedra sinica*, which yields ephedrine, a drug still used to treat asthma and bronchitis. Another famous Chinese medical herb is ginseng (*Panax pseudoginseng*).

Acupuncture was first practiced more than 4,500 years ago. Chinese scientists were forbidden to dissect bodies, so they had no accurate knowledge of anatomy. They believed the body contained three "burning spaces" and that yin and yang circulate through 12 channels. Acupuncture aims to alter the distribution of yin and yang in the body by inserting metal needles of varying lengths into the skin at points on the body that are related to the organ or organs that are sick.

Ayurvedic medicine is based on religious writings called the "Vedas." It is still used in India, where it probably originated about 3,000 years ago. Its aim is to prevent illness through modifications of lifestyle, improved hygiene, and the practice of yoga, and to cure complaints by using herbal and mineral preparations and a correct diet. Ayurvedic practitioners treat the whole person rather than simply dealing with a particular illness.

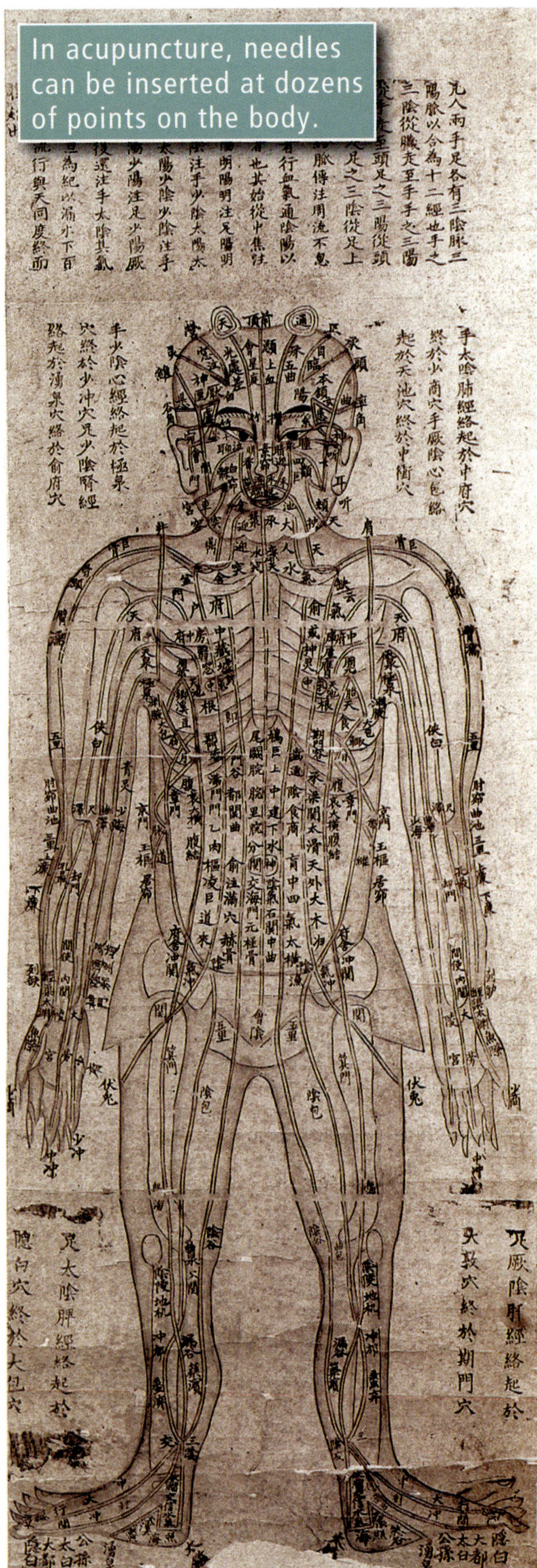

In acupuncture, needles can be inserted at dozens of points on the body.

ACTIVITIES

Video

What Is Acupuncture?

Watch the video to learn more about acupuncture.

1. What does the speaker say acupuncture is to acupuncturists? List the other methods the speaker describes that have the same effect as acupuncture.
2. What does the speaker say the key to acupuncture is? What is the thickness of the needles used in acupuncture? What analogy does he use to describe the effect of the needles?

Weblink

Why Our Ancestors Drilled Holes in Each Other's Skulls

Read the link to learn more about trepanning.

1. What medical conditions might ancient peoples have used trepanning to treat? Describe the other purpose that researchers think trepanning may have had. When does the earliest clear evidence of trepanation date from?
2. Explain why it is difficult to say for certain that trepanning was not used for a medical condition. Where has good evidence for ritual trepanation been found? Describe what was unusual about the finds.
3. What reason does one researcher give for the trepanations being performed in specific, dangerous areas of the skull? What evidence is there that the majority of the patients survived the trepanning for years after the operation?

RUBRIC

Analyzing a Primary Source

Students will complete a thorough analysis of a primary source. An exemplary analysis will meet the following criteria:

- Identifies the creator of the source
- Explains what medium was used to create the primary source
- Describes why the source qualifies as a primary one
- Explores any literary devices used in the source
- Identifies the intended audience for the source
- Relates the creator's goals in creating the source
- Illustrates knowledge of the period and location in which the source was created
- Distinguishes between facts and opinions found in the source
- Examines the reliability of the source's creator
- Compares the source with similar documents
- Cites additional sources used in the analysis
- Presents information in a clear, concise manner
- Uses correct spelling, grammar, and punctuation

The pyramids on the Giza Plateau in Egypt were once coated in smooth, pale limestone.

Building the Pyramids

Four thousand years ago, the only way people knew to build a tall structure was with a broad base tapering to a point. Smooth-sided pyramids were a progression from step pyramids, or ziggurats. Ziggurats were built from bricks in Mesopotamia and Persia between 3000 and 500 BC. A ziggurat was built in levels, each smaller than the one below. It may have represented a sacred mountain or a link between Earth and heaven.

Refining The Design

The first pyramid in Egypt was built at Saqqara, starting in about 2630 BC, to honor King Djoser. It had a stepped structure like that of a ziggurat, but was made of stone rather than bricks. Within 30 years, the Egyptians had refined the design and were building smooth pyramids, such as the Red Pyramid at Dashur, considered the first "true" pyramid. The core was made from massive structural stone blocks, but they were cased in smaller blocks to make the outline of the structure appear smoother.

The pyramids were burial structures built to honor the kings, or pharaohs, who were regarded by their people as living gods. The site for a pyramid was chosen by the king himself. Detailed plans were drawn up by skilled draftsmen working on sheets of papyrus. Sometimes, the pyramids were built over rocky outcrops that formed the core of the structure.

Building above natural rocks meant fewer materials had to be imported. Uneven ground is more difficult to survey and measure, however, and precision was imperative. Egyptian pyramids are built along a north–south axis. The builders determined the direction of true north from the stars and used geometry to mark out the base of the pyramid as a perfect square. If they were inaccurate, the four sides would fail to form a point at the apex. The same perfection was required of the individual blocks, which were shaped by skilled masons.

Estimates of the numbers of people involved in building the pyramids vary from 100,000 to just a few thousand. It seems unlikely that these people were slaves. There is archaeological evidence of thriving communities centered on the construction sites, providing accommodation and services for a huge, highly specialized workforce.

One estimate is that it took 100,000 workers 20 years to build a pyramid.

A Greek in Egypt

The ancient Greek Herodotus wrote an account of a visit to Egypt in the first half of the early 300s BC. The account includes the first written descriptions of the pyramids and of Egyptian religion. Herodotus reported that the Great Pyramid took 20 years to build, plus another 10 years for the causeway that linked the pyramid to the Nile River. He also said that the Egyptians used "machines" to raise stone blocks to build pyramids, but did not provide any more information about the nature of these devices. Today, historians know that Herodotus was wrong in many facts he claimed to have been told by priests in Egypt during his short visit. He spoke no Egyptian and did not read hieroglyphs, so he could only gather a limited amount of information. Still, Herodotus has a reputation as the world's first historian, even though he mainly wrote down stories he heard.

ACTIVITIES

First Hand

Herodotus: The SecondBook of the Histories, Called Euterpe
Read Herodotus' account of the building of the pyramids

1. What materials does Herodotus say the Egyptians used to build their boats? Research online to discover the imperial and metric equivalents for the ancient measurements of talents, furlongs, and fathoms.
2. Herodotus says it took 100,000 workers 20 years to build the Great Pyramid. What do historians today estimate is a more likely figure? Evaluate whether the reliability of Herodotus' text is compromised because it contains errors. Say why or why not.
3. Describe what Herodotus says is written on the side of the pyramids. How much does he report this has cost?

Weblink

Pyramid Construction
Examine the weblink to learn more about the construction of the pyramids.

1. What are the three theories of how the pyramids were constructed? Describe in your own words how these methods work. Explain why one of the theories has been disputed.
2. Explain why it is unlikely that slave labor was used to build the pyramids. Which people do scholars think are the likely builders? Research online to find evidence of this theory.
3. What are the other structures that are associated with pyramids in a funerary complex?

The First Boats

The dugout canoe was the first purpose-built boat. It was made from a log hollowed out using an ax or an adz, which is an ax with the blade set at right angles to the shaft. Next, boatbuilders learned to make a canoe by stretching leather or bark over a light wooden framework, using resin or bitumen to help make it watertight. Native American bark canoes and Welsh coracles still use this type of lightweight construction.

The first boats were propelled by oars. Sails were the next development. They were invented by the Egyptians for the boats that sailed on the Nile River in about 3500 BC. Sails allowed boats to be pushed along by the wind.

Sail Development

At first, Egyptian boat hulls were made from woven papyrus reeds. By about 4000 BC, boatbuilders used wooden planks bound together with strips of leather or papyrus. The first sailboats were square-rigged, so they had a square sail set at right angles to the direction of travel. They were fine for traveling in the same direction as the wind, and were used for centuries by the Egyptians, other Mediterranean peoples, and the Vikings of northern Europe. The boat was steered using one or two long oars over the stern. The sail was usually wider than it was tall and could be angled slightly using ropes attached to yards at the top and bottom of the sail. There were raised lookout positions in the bow and stern and a deckhouse for passengers in the center.

Full-sized boats were buried near Egyptian pyramids. They may have been intended to help the spirit of the dead cross the sky to join the gods.

Dhows are still used by fishers and for transportation on the Nile River.

170
ROWERS
The number of oarsmen on a Greek trireme in the 600s BC.

125
ELEPHANTS
The equivalent weight carried by an Egyptian cargo ship (500 tons/453 metric tons).

Some of the boats were very large. A highly decorated dismantled boat found buried near a tomb dating from about 2500 BC was 140 feet (43 m) long and constructed from more than 1,200 separate pieces of cedar wood. Later Egyptian vessels abandoned sails and reverted to banks of oars for propulsion. By about 700 BC, the Phoenicians were using vessels known as biremes that had two banks of oars. By about 650 BC, Mediterranean peoples used triremes with three banks of oars.

Adding Maneuverability

In the first century AD, Chinese boatbuilders invented the rudder, a pivoted vertical plank that is an integral part of the boat. They also invented so-called mat-and-batten sails, in which each mast has a set of sails separated by horizontal battens, or yards. This arrangement is still used on Chinese junks. Another major breakthrough was the triangular lateen sail, invented in the third century by Arabian sailors. A lateen sail can be swung around to allow the vessel to sail closer to the wind. This means that the wind does not have to come from directly behind the ship for it to be able to make reasonable progress. Most dhows today still carry triangular sails. The Arabs used similar vessels to explore the eastern coast of Africa south to the Cape of Good Hope and possibly beyond.

Exploring the Oceans

Mediterranean vessels also adopted lateen sails, often in combination with square sails on the main masts. For example, a caravel has four masts with square sails on the first two masts and triangular sails on the other two. It was the descendants of these craft that later Spanish and Portuguese navigators used for their epic voyages of exploration in the fifteenth and sixteenth centuries, becoming the first vessels to circumnavigate the globe.

ACTIVITIES

Video

Salvaging a 5,000-year-old Boat in Egypt

Examine the video to learn more about an ancient craft in Egypt.

1. What percentage of Egyptians live along the Nile? Explain why this is the case.
2. How long does it take archaeologists to retrieve a single plank? Explain why it is such a slow and painstaking process. When was the first boat found at the Great Pyramid site excavated?
3. Why did the ancient Egyptians bury boats with the pharaohs? Research online what other objects the ancient Egyptians buried with the dead.

Weblink

History of Ships: Prehistoric Craft

Read the article to learn more about prehistoric craft.

1. What is the oldest discovered boat in the world? When does it date from?
2. What evidence does the writer provide to support the theory that Homo erectus built seaworthy craft? How long before modern humans developed does the writer propose this took place?
3. List the three main categories of prehistoric craft. What type of craft was Thor Heyerdahl's Kon-Tiki? Describe the main objective of his expedition in 1947.

RUBRIC

Creating a Map

Students will create a map detailing a topic or event. An exemplary map will meet the following criteria:

- Title tells the purpose/content of the map, is clearly distinguishable as the title (e.g. larger letters, underlined, etc.)
- All items are labeled and located correctly
- Legend is easy to find and contains a complete set of symbols, including a compass rose
- All features on map are drawn to scale and the scale used is clearly indicated on the map
- All words on the map are spelled and capitalized correctly
- Student always uses color appropriate for features (e.g. blue for water; black for labels, etc.) on map
- Map includes properly documented sources

Using Metals

The first metals were "native." They could be found lying on the surface of the ground or in the sand of riverbeds. These metals include gold, silver, and copper. The first metal used for a practical purpose was copper. Gold and silver could be shaped by hammering, or mixed to make a metal called electrum.

Copper

When introduced: c.5000 BC

Where introduced: Egypt

Sources: Nuggets or in rocks

Uses: Weapons, tools, helmets, vessels

Alloys: Bronze (copper and tin)

Advantages: Occurs naturally, harder than gold and silver for tools, bronze keeps sharp edge for longer

Drawbacks: Requires melting and casting into shapes, loses sharpness quickly if not alloyed with tin

Gold and Silver

When introduced: c.3000 BC (gold), c.4000 BC (silver)

Where introduced: Sumer and Egypt (gold), Greece and Anatolia (silver)

Sources: Nuggets or in rocks

Uses: Jewelry, plates and cups, masks, ornaments, ceremonial weapons

Alloys: Electrum (silver and gold)

Advantages: Occur naturally, easy to shape, beautiful appearance

Drawbacks: Too soft to have practical uses

ACTIVITIES

However, they are too soft to make tools or weapons. Later, people mixed tin with copper to create bronze, which was much harder than copper. Another useful metal was iron, which required high temperatures to extract it from its ore. Steel was a harder metal, but needed even higher temperatures to make.

Iron

When introduced: 2200 BC
Where introduced: Turkey
Sources: Meteorites, hematite (iron ore)
Uses: Weapons, ceremonial objects, tools
Alloys: Steel (iron and carbon)
Advantages: Valuable, can be turned into steel
Drawbacks: Rare to find, requires high temperatures for smelting, difficult to work, creates soft artifacts

Carbon Steel

When introduced: c.1800 BC
Where introduced: Turkey
Sources: Alloy of iron and carbon
Uses: Bladed tools and weapons
Variations: Wootz steel
Advantages: Remains sharp during use, strengthened by plunging red-hot steel into cold water
Drawbacks: Too expensive to make for everyday use

More

Using Metals

Research online to learn more about copper, gold and silver, iron, and carbon steel.

1. Did early people use any other metals? Compare and contrast the different metals, listing their advantages and drawbacks.
2. The discovery of metals played a large part in the development of human civilization. Analyze which of the metals was the most significant for civilization. Explain your answer.

The Moon takes about 29.5 days to go through its cycle from new Moon to new Moon.

Calendars

In the 1970s, scientists excavating a cave in Swaziland discovered a baboon's leg bone. Now called the Lebombo bone, it was marked with 29 notches. The person who made those marks lived about 35,000 years ago, and the marks may record the passage of time. If so, this is a 'calendar stick,' similar to those made quite recently by Native American people.

Following the Moon

The Lebombo bone is not the only example of an early calendar from Africa. On the shores of Lake Edward in the Democratic Republic of Congo there was once a small community. It created the Ishango bone, discovered in 1960 and named for the people who made it. Notches on the bone count the days in the lunar cycle, from **new Moon** to new Moon, over a period of six months. The bone dates from 25,000 years ago. There are good reasons for predicting the phases of the Moon. Hunters have enough light to hunt during the full Moon, and warriors can approach their enemies unnoticed on moonless nights. People have also always needed to count the passage of time.

Building a Calendar

All early calendars were based on the lunar cycle. The Egyptians were probably the first people to develop a calendar for a whole year, in about 4236 BC. The lunar calendar failed to predict the most important event in the Egyptian year, the annual flooding of the River Nile.

The Nile flood was linked to the seasons. Egyptian priest-astronomers found that, when the star Sirius was visible shortly before sunrise, the Nile flooded a few days later. The astronomers devised a calendar based on a solar year and lunar months. It had three seasons, each made up of four months of 30 days. There were five extra days at the end of the year, making a year of 365 days. The Egyptians also used a unit of time longer than a year. This measurement was the reign of a king, or pharaoh. They counted years as "year such-and-such of king so-and-so."

The Egyptians were the first people to divide the day into 24 units. These units were not the same as hours, however, because they were not of equal length. There were 12 daytime units and 12 nighttime units. Their lengths changed with the length of the day and night through the seasons.

The Aztec carved huge stones to record the calendar.

260
DAYS
The number of days in the ancient Mayan calendar, which is still used by peoples in South America.

94
YEARS
Said to be the reign of the longest-ruling Egyptian king, Pepi II.

The Sumerians

By about 3000 BC, the Sumerian calendar divided the year into 12 months of 30 days each. There were 12 periods in a day, and each period was divided into 30 parts. Months began with the appearance of the new Moon, and the new year began at the time of the barley harvest. The financial year began about two months later, when the harvested grain was sent to market.

The Aztec

The Aztec and other American peoples had two calendars. One was used for agricultural events such as planting and harvesting. The other was used to carry out rituals. The agricultural calendar was based on the seasons and divided the year into 365 days. The ritual calendar had 260 days. The Aztec followed both calendars simultaneously. The calendars coincided once every 52 years, in an Aztec "century."

ACTIVITIES

Weblink

A Walk through Time: Ancient Calendars
Review the weblink to learn more about ancient calendars.

1. What do the alignments of Stonehenge, in England, show about its probable purposes?
2. How many days did the Babylonian months have? How many days were in the Babylonian year?
3. What celestial bodies did the Maya rely on to create their calendars? When did they believe the world had been created?

Weights and Measures

In the ancient world, each culture had its own system of weights and measures. People based early measures of length on parts of the body. The Egyptian cubit measured about 18 inches (45 centimeters). It was the distance from the elbow to the tip of the first finger. It was used from 3500 BC. The ancient Greek cubit of 1,500 years later was based on the length of an average adult's foot. It measured about 12 inches (30 cm). The foot (30.5 cm) is still used, and the hand (4 inches, or 10.2 cm) is used to measure the height of a horse. The word "inch" comes from the Latin *uncia*, meaning a twelfth part of a foot.

Weight

Units of weight have no convenient natural object to act as a standard. Grains, based on grains of wheat or rice, were used to weigh small amounts. Carats, based on the size of beans, are still used to measure precious metals. A grain equals 0.0012 ounces (0.05 grams), and there are four grains in a carat. In about 2500 BC, Sumerian traders made an attempt to standardize weights.

The Egyptians believed the god Anubis weighed the hearts of the dead in a balance against a feather.

Ancient Weights and Measures

Early farmers, craftsmen, engineers, and scientists needed to establish relationships for quantities and dimensions in order to record them. There were no universal systems of weights and measures, however. Many lengths were based on the human body, such as the foot, but those measurements varied widely. Standards for weight were even more difficult to find. Different units of measurement were adopted by different early civilizations.

UNIT	COUNTRY	MEASUREMENT	MODERN EQUIVALENT	
			(Imperial)	(Metric)
acetabulum	Rome	volume	2.24 fluid ounces	66.41 milliliters
actus	Rome	area	1,519 sq. yards	0.127 hectares
amphora	Greece	volume	10.26 gallons	38.84 liters
brachium	Rome	length	4.6 feet	1.4 meters
cab	Israel	volume	4.73 pints	2.24 liters
cubit	Egypt	length	17.76 inches	45.11 centimeters
digit	Egypt	length	0.74 inches	18.72 millimeters
foot	Babylon	length	13.93 inches	35.4 centimeters
khoinix	Greece	dry volume	0.98 quarts	1,079 cubic centimeters
libra	Rome	weight	1.01 pounds	459.26 grams
ligula	Rome	volume	0.39 fluid ounces	11.67 milliliters
mile	Rome	length	1,618 yards	1,479.5 meters
mina	Sumeria	weight	17.7 ounces	504 grams
palm	Egypt	length	2.95 inches	7.49 centimeters
royal cubit	Egypt	length	20.64 inches	52.42 centimeters
shekel	Sumeria	weight	0.3 ounces	8.4 grams

The digit and the palm were later adopted by ancient Israel, Greece, and Rome with almost exactly the same dimensions. Cubits were also used in Babylon, Israel, Greece, and Rome, and all had similar values.

They introduced the shekel, which weighed about 0.3 ounces (8.4 g) and the mina, equal to 60 shekels. The oldest surviving weight dates from 2400 BC in Mesopotamia. About 500 years later, authorities in Nippur in Sumer used a copper bar as a standard of both length and weight. The Romans used the *libra pondo*, pound by weight, equal to about 16 ounces (460 g). Libra is the origin of the abbreviation “lb” for pound.

Standards for volume measurement were often based on storage vessels. One was the amphora, a jar used in Greece and Rome for storing oil or wine. Other units have derived from various barrels and bottles used for wine. Today, champagne bottles form a series in which each volume is double the size of the previous one. Their names are based on the Old Testament—magnum, jeroboam, rehoboam, methuselah, and balthazar.

ACTIVITIES

Transparency

Ancient Weights and Measures

Examine the chart and research online to learn more about ancient weights and measures.

1. Why might ancient peoples have used parts of the body to measure length? Explain why standards for length varied widely. Why was it more difficult to find standards of weight?
2. Analyze why having different units of measurement in different civilizations may have led to problems with trade. How might ancient peoples have overcome these difficulties?

Weblink

Measuring Length in Ancient Egypt

Review the weblink to learn more about measuring length in ancient Egypt.

1. How long is a river-unit? What is an early source for this measure?
2. List the other divisions that have been found on cubit rods. Describe what these units might have been used to measure.

RUBRIC

Analyzing a Magazine Article

Students will assess a magazine article and write an analysis. An exemplary analysis will meet the following criteria.

- Identifies the topic of the article
- Identifies the main points and opinions presented in the article
- Identifies the writer of the article
- Presents information about the writer and infers how his or her life may have shaped this opinion
- Assesses the writer's reliability
- Analyzes how the writer makes his or her argument
- Uses evidence from the article to show how the writer supports his or her argument
- Analyzes the writer's use of literary devices to enhance the article
- Differentiates between the facts and opinions presented in the article
- Identifies when and where the article was published, and determines its intended audience
- Identifies and understands the goals of the article
- Assesses the effectiveness of the format in presenting the writer's argument
- Connects the article to the societal and historical context in which it was written
- Infers what is not said about this topic in the article
- Identifies what information is unintentionally implied in the article

The tholos, or circular shrine, built at Delphi in about 390 BC originally had 20 large pillars around the outside.

Greek Temples and Tombs

In ancient Greece, the development of construction technology was closely linked to religion. The Greeks believed that their gods lived in places known as sanctuaries, such as woodland groves, mountaintops, or caves. These sites became the locations of shrines with altars where worshippers could leave offerings. Some sanctuaries were medical centers that provided healing.

Some sanctuaries had an oracle, a person through whom the god offered advice to visitors. The most famous oracle was the Pythia at the shrine to Apollo at Delphi. Most oracles occupied chambers below ground, but the Pythia sat on a tripod stool in a low room. The first shrine at Delphi was destroyed by fire in 548 BC. It was rebuilt with accommodation for priests and officials. Other shrines also grew into more substantial collections of buildings.

Building Temples

When the Greeks began to represent their gods with large statues, the statues were protected from the weather in buildings called naoi, or "dwellings." The first structures were wood and mud brick, but they were later built in stone and brick. The buildings were rectangular, with an entrance porch at one end covered with a roof supported by columns.

Later temples had a porch at either end and were surrounded by columns. The first-known example of a temple surrounded by columns is the Temple of Hera (Heraion) at Samos, built in 750 BC. Another temple of Hera, at Olympia, was built in about 600 BC. It originally had wooden columns, but they were later replaced in stone. There were 6 columns at each end and 16 columns along each side.

The Parthenon, built of white marble on the hill of the Acropolis at Athens, is the largest and most famous of all Greek temples. It was built under the supervision of the Greek sculptor Phidias. Work began in 447 BC, and the building was completed in 438 BC, although the exterior decoration was not finished until 432 BC. The Parthenon was dedicated to Athena Parthenos (Athena the Virgin) and contained a massive statue of her.

Roman Greece

In 146 BC, Greece became part of the Roman Empire. When Christianity became the official religion of Rome in 380 AD, various emperors sought to stamp out the pagan Greek religion. Theodosius I (347–395) banned the Olympic Games in 394, but otherwise the imperial edicts had little effect. The Greeks held on to their traditional beliefs. Little by little the Greeks converted, however, and their temples gradually became Christian churches. The Parthenon became a Byzantine church and then a Roman Catholic church. The Temple of Athena at Syracuse, Sicily, built between 474 and 460 BC, was made into a Christian church in 640 AD, and is now a cathedral. The Temple of Concord, built in the fifth century BC at what is now Agrigento, Sicily, became a church in 597 AD.

The gold-and-ivory statue of Athena in the Parthenon was 40 feet (12.1 m) tall.

ACTIVITIES

Document

Temple of Athena Nike

Read the document to learn more about the Temple of Athena Nike on the Acropolis in Athens, Greece.

1. When was the temple constructed? In what style are its columns? Who was Athena? What is the name of the architect who is said to have built the temple?
2. Research online to learn more about the battles of the Gigantomachy and the Amazonomachy. Explain why the architect decorated the temple with sculptures of battle scenes.
3. Some of these sculptures are today housed in the British Museum in London as part of the Elgin Marbles collection. Greece has long campaigned for their return. Evaluate whether the sculptures should be returned to Greece or whether they should stay with the British Museum. Give reasons for your answer.

Weblink

Ancient Greek Architecture and the Greek Seven Wonders

Read the weblink to learn more about ancient Greek architecture.

1. Describe the main difference between Egyptian and Greek temples. Identify one reason why this was the case.
2. Describe the main differences between Ionic and Dorian columns. What building is considered to be the quintessential Doric structure? How do Corinthian columns differ from the other types?
3. What were the main influences on Greek architecture? What does the text say was one of the great contributions of Greek architecture?

Simple Machines

Early peoples used simple machines to replace or increase muscle power. The machines enabled them to do more work, more easily. In the first century AD, the Greek inventor Hero of Alexandria described five simple machines. They are the **lever**, the wheel and axle, the pulley, the ramp, and the screw.

Shadoof

Purpose: Raising buckets of water for irrigation

Type of machine: Lever

Principle: Turns a small force into a large one by using a **fulcrum**

When invented: c.2500 BC

Where invented: Mesopotamia

Advantages: Enables a human operator to raise heavy volumes of water

Waterwheel

Purpose: Turning water flow into circular motion for tasks such as grinding corn

Type of machine: Wheel

Principle: Uses toothed gears to change speed of rotation or twisting power, or torque, of a power source

When invented: c.300s BC

Where invented: Greece

Advantages: Continuous supply of energy, can be adapted to range of tasks

ACTIVITIES

Ancient engineers used variations on these five simple machines to build a wide range of devices. Many machines were linked with agriculture, such as means of moving water for **irrigation**. Others were linked to grinding grains into flour or making utensils for storage.

Potter's Wheel

Purpose: Providing circular motion to help manufacture smooth pots

Type of machine: Wheel

Principle: Converts up-and-down action of treadle into rotary action

When invented: c.3500 BC

Where invented: Turkey

Advantages: Allows pots to be made with thin walls, making them lighter and easier to use as a means of storage

Archimedes Screw

Purpose: Raising water for irrigation

Type of machine: Screw

Principle: Cylindrical shaft with spiral thread around the outside converts circular motion to linear motion

When invented: c.300s BC

Where invented: Egypt, Greece

Advantages: Raises constant stream of water for irrigation

More

Simple Machines

Research online to learn more about the shadoof, waterwheel, potter's wheel, and Archimedes screw.

1. Compare and contrast the four simple machines. Analyze which of the four has been the most significant for the development of human civilization. Justify your answer.
2. Which of these early machines are still used in largely unchanged form today? Describe examples.

Weblink

The classic six simple machines

Read the weblink to learn more about simple machines.

1. What is the sixth simple machine referred to here? Define mechanical advantage.
2. Describe the two classes in which simple machines can be placed. To which class does Archimedes screw belong? Infer to what class the shadoof belongs.
3. Describe how the mechanical advantage of an inclined can be realized. What is the cost? Explain what is meant by an inclined plane with a gradient of 1:12?

RUBRIC

Analyzing a Scientific Biography

Students will research the life of a scientific figure and present their findings. An exemplary biographical analysis will meet the following criteria:

- Illustrates strong knowledge of the subject
- Identifies the author of the biography
- Describes why the subject of the biography is important
- Contains information about the time and place in which the subject was born
- Lists important events in the subject's life
- Explains how events in the subject's life impacted him or her
- Makes inferences about the subject based on events in his or her life
- Explains how the subject influenced the world while he or she lived
- Researches the cultural and historical context of the subject's life
- Examines the effect that the subject has had on the modern world
- Supplements information from the biography with independent research
- Organizes the analysis in a logical, effective manner
- Uses correct spelling, grammar, and punctuation
- Cites all sources used in the analysis

The claw was said to be able to lift a heavy ship almost upright before dropping it onto rocks to smash.

Archimedes' Inventions

Archimedes was the greatest mathematician and physicist of the ancient world. He was born in about 287 BC in the Greek colony of Syracuse in Sicily. Archimedes later studied in Alexandria, Egypt, before returning to Syracuse, where he remained for the rest of his life.

Archimedes was the first person to work out the principle underlying levers. He claimed that, with a lever long and strong enough, he could move the world. This claim led King Hieron of Syracuse to challenge Archimedes to move a very heavy object. Archimedes is said to have assembled a system of levers and pulleys with which Hieron himself was able to pull a fully laden ship out of the dry dock, across land, and into the harbor. Archimedes is said to have designed a **planetarium** and also the screw pump to help with irrigation of crops. This is a spiral screw inside a cylinder which, when turned, raises water. It is still used today.

Fearsome Weapons

Archimedes also invented weapons to defend Syracuse from a Roman siege in 215 BC. Hieron asked Archimedes to design defenses for the city. It involved rebuilding the walls to hold powerful catapults, cranes that lifted large boulders and dropped them onto the enemy, and several novel weapons.

Archimedes' weapons held the invaders at bay for three years. Among the most fearsome of the weapons were the "claws of Archimedes." They would descend onto any ship that came within range and shake it violently or even lift it high into the air and swing it until all the soldiers were shaken out of it. No one knows exactly how the claws worked, but the device may have been a large hook lowered by a tall crane. Legend also tells of a focusing mirror that worked as a burning glass. It was said that it set fire to the sails of any ship that approached close enough.

The Romans finally took Syracuse in about 212 BC. The general, Marcellus, ordered that Archimedes should not be harmed. A Roman soldier found Archimedes doing some mathematical work. When the soldier demanded that Archimedes accompany him, the mathematician told him not to disturb the circles he had drawn in the sand. Impatient, the soldier killed him.

There is no evidence that the burning glass actually existed.

A Eureka Moment

Archimedes's inventions to defend Syracuse were recorded by the Greek historian Polybius. Polybius lived nearly a century after Archimedes, so his account may not be reliable. Another story recounts that King Hieron asked Archimedes if his new crown was pure gold or whether the gold had been mixed with cheaper silver, as he suspected. Archimedes could not think of how to test this until one day his bath overflowed. He realized that when an object is immersed in water, it displaces its own volume of water. Archimedes measured the volume of the crown by immersing it in water. He then measured a piece of gold weighing the same as the crown in the same way. Silver is less dense than gold, and bulkier. When the crown displaced more water than the same weight of pure gold, Archimedes could tell the king that the goldsmith had cheated him.

ACTIVITIES

First Hand

Histories by Polybius, Archimedes

Read the extract from Polybius's Histories.

1. Describe the defenses Archimedes used when the Roman ships came close to land. What reason does the translator give in the footnote for the name "scorpion"?
2. Sambucae were engines for storming city walls. How does Polybius describe Archimedes' attack on them?
3. Polybius says some of the stones on Archimedes' machines weighed 10 talents. Calculate what this weight is in pounds.

Weblink

How Archimedes Took on the Romans

Read the article to learn more about the inventions of Archimedes.

1. What does the writer of this article say Archimedes should be given more credit for? Do you agree with his argument? Give reasons for your answer.
2. Describe how Archimedes improved the design of Syracuse's catapults. Explain the type of simple machine that Archimedes used in his claw.
3. What did the Roman commander Marcellus say about Archimedes? Infer what he meant by his comment. Explain why Marcellus wanted to take Archimedes alive. Give reasons for your answer.

Ancient India

About 1500 BC, Aryan people began migrating southwestward into the broad plain of the Ganga, or Ganges, River, in what is now northern India. There were many fierce battles, in which Aryan tribes defeated the people already occupying the land. The Aryans were primarily **pastoralists** and farmers. They settled in villages and tilled the land

The Aryans eventually established Indo-Aryan kingdoms, where the Brahman religion and the Sanskrit language developed. Dynasties rose and fell, boundaries shifted, and in about 321 BC Chandragupta Maurya became the first ruler of the Mauryan Dynasty. Chandragupta greatly expanded the empire.

Rice was the staple food of the people living along the Ganges. Archaeologists have found charred rice grains in Bihar in northeast India dating from 2000 to 1500 BC. Rice also became the most important crop grown by the Aryan farmers.

There are two ways to grow rice. On sloping ground in the hills, rice is grown as a field crop, watered by the rain. In the lowlands, it is raised in seedbeds and transplanted into flooded fields called paddies, which are drained before harvesting. Paddy rice produces bigger yields than upland rice, but its successful cultivation depends on careful management of the water supply. Water management is especially important in India's monsoon climate, where nearly all the rain falls during the summer.

In hilly regions, people built steplike terraces into hillsides to make paddy fields. The terraces made more flat land available for growing crops.

Canals and Irrigation

Dams, artificial lakes, and irrigation systems were being used by the 300s BC. Some of the irrigation schemes used rainwater or floodwater that had been harvested and stored. Inundation canals were widely used in Bengal, in northeast India. These broad, shallow canals were opened when meltwater from the mountains combined with the monsoon rains to raise river levels. Water rich in silt flowed along the canals and into smaller channels leading to the fields. Once the river level began to fall, the main canals were closed.

Ahar-pyne was a similar system developed on sloping ground in Bihar. Pynes are channels leading from the river to an ahar, which is a rectangular basin enclosed by embankments on three sides. The natural slope of the land forms the fourth side of the basin. A tank built in the first century BC at Sringaverapura near Allahabad in northern India is a remarkable example of water harvesting. It is 800 feet (244 m) long, 60 feet (18 m) wide, and 12 feet (3.7 m) deep and lined with brick. Water from the Ganges flowed downhill and through two deep earthen tanks, where silt settled to the bottom. Water left each of these tanks from outlets near the top. As it entered the main tank, the water passed over steps between curved walls that slowed the flow. To make sure water was available in the dry season, several wells were dug in the bottom of the tank.

Metalworking

Indian technology continued to advance. In the grounds of the Quwwat-ul-Islam Mosque in the Mehrauli area of Delhi, stands a cast-iron pillar that is over 23.5 feet (7 m) tall and 16 inches (40 cm) in diameter. It weighs more than 6.6 tons (5.9 metric tons). The iron pillar was erected in 415 AD during the classical period in Indian history that began with the founding of the Gupta Dynasty in 320 AD.

The pillar was commissioned by the king Kumara Gupta in honor of his father, Chandra Gupta II. It is inscribed with accounts of Chandra Gupta's military exploits. It was not until some 1,400 years later, in the nineteenth century, that European ironworkers were capable of casting a single piece of metal the size of Kumara's iron pillar.

Kumara's iron pillar has not rusted despite being exposed to the weather for 1,500 years.

ACTIVITIES

Video

Growing Rice in India.
Examine the video to learn more about growing rice in India.

1. Describe where the transplantation method is used. Explain how most farmers ensure there is sufficient water to plant rice in their fields.
2. Explain the method of transplanting rice. Why is it described as "difficult"?
3. Where is rice grown in upland areas? How are the rice crops harvested? Infer what method farmers use to harvest rice crops in upland areas.

Weblink

Metalwork in South Asia
Review the article on metalwork in South Asia.

1. The text says "India iron immediately succeeded stone as a material for tools and weapons." What can you infer from this statement?
2. Where have gold and silver drinking vessels and jewelry of Hellenistic types been excavated? What evidence does the text cite for the production of vessels of Hellenistic and Persian shapes in the Gupta period?
3. Analyze why no original pieces of jewelry have survived. Describe where Indian jewelry can be studied today.

RUBRIC

Creating a Timeline

Students will explore a topic related to an event and create a timeline to present their research on historical events connected to this topic. An exemplary timeline will meet the following criteria:

- Includes the most significant events pertaining to the topic to be compared and analyzed
- Includes interesting events
- Uses accurate information for all events, including date, location, and major details
- Orders the events in a chronological sequence
- Describes each event with accurate, vivid, and specific details
- Presents the topic from three or more perspectives
- Inspires the reader to ask thoughtful questions regarding the events and perspectives presented in the timeline
- Uses correct spelling, grammar, and punctuation
- Presents the timeline in a visually attractive and striking manner
- Presents the timeline in a neat, organized manner that is logical and easy to follow
- Uses creativity to present the timeline in an engaging manner
- Effectively communicates historical information relating to the topic
- Supports each event with reliable sources
- Includes a correctly formatted bibliography of all sources used to create the timeline

Roman Roads and Aqueducts

From the fourth century BC, the Romans built roads throughout their empire. At their peak, Roman roads stretched over 50,000 miles (80,000 km), enough to pass twice around the world. There were 29 great military roads spreading out from Rome. There was a system from Carthage in North Africa that ran along the southern coast of the Mediterranean Sea. In Gaul, or France, roads radiated from Lyon, and in Britain, London was the hub of the road system. The first Roman road was the Appian Way, built southward from Rome in 312 BC. At first, the Appian Way ran only as far as Capua, but it was later extended to the coast at Brundisium, or Brindisi.

Other roads soon followed, such as the Via Aurelia to Genoa and the Via Flaminia to the Adriatic coast. The Romans built roads mainly so that couriers, merchants, and officials such as tax collectors could travel more easily. The roads were also useful for moving troops rapidly in case of trouble with the local people.

A Roman Road

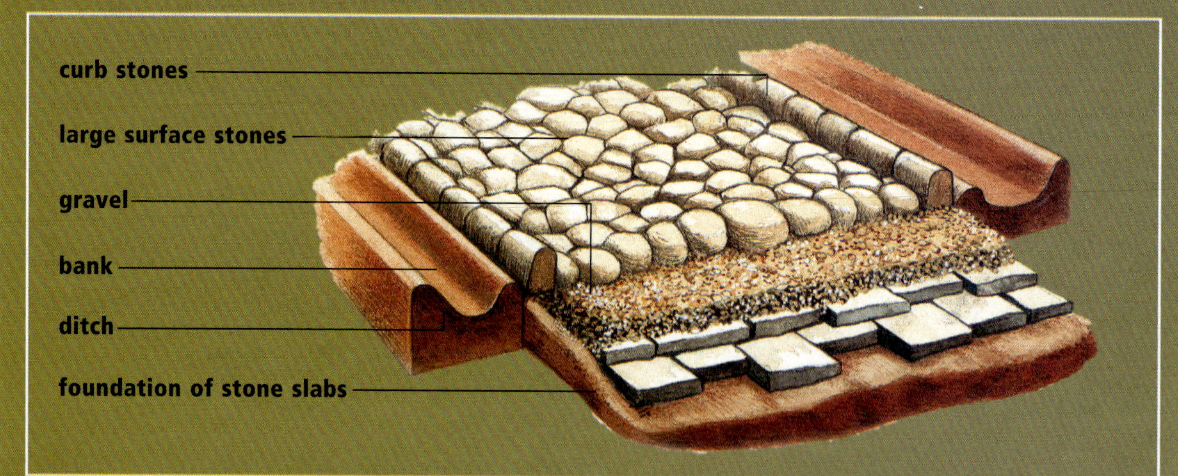

To construct a major highway, Roman engineers first dug parallel drainage ditches about 40 feet (12 m) apart. They then excavated a shallow trench between the ditches, which they filled with sand, mortar, and a succession of stone courses to form the foundation of the road. They topped a watertight layer of crushed stone with a surface pavement of stone slabs or cobbles set in mortar. They made concrete from crushed stones, volcanic ash cement called pozzolana, if it was available, and lime. On marshy ground, the whole road was raised above the surrounding countryside.

Road Construction

Wherever possible, Roman roads followed a straight line set out by surveyors using a sighting staff called a groma. If roads had to turn, they tended to turn at high points where there was a wide field of view. Some of the major roads in Italy had stone curbs 8 inches (20 cm) high and 2 feet (60 cm) wide on each side. There were side lanes outside the curbs that operated as one-way streets. Drivers of fast two-wheeled chariots could achieve 75 miles (120 km) a day along these roads, although eight-horse freight wagons covered a more modest 15 miles (25 km) a day.

As the Roman Empire crumbled in the late 400s AD, so did its roads, due to a lack of maintenance. Later road builders sometimes took over the Roman routes. The original routes can still be identified by the arrow-straight stretches on any road map of England.

Water Supplies

As Roman towns and cities grew in size, there was an increasing demand for water for people to drink and to wash in. Public baths and fountains were features of many Roman towns. To bring in the water, engineers built aqueducts, which are permanent channels for carrying water. It may be an open or closed culvert, a tunnel through a hill, or a viaduct across a valley.

Between 312 BC and 200 AD, Roman engineers built 11 aqueducts just to take water into Rome, some from more than 56 miles (90 km) away. They constructed the aqueducts with a gentle downward slope, and the water flowed by gravity. Other Roman aqueducts in Italy, Greece, and Spain are still used.

The aqueduct at Segovia, Spain, was built by Emperor Trajan. It is made from 24,000 granite blocks fitted together without mortar to form a 2,400-foot (730-m) series of 165 arches. The three-tiered arches of the famous Pont du Gard near Nîmes, France, extend for 900 feet (275 m) and reach a height of 165 feet (50 m). It was built in about 20 BC by Roman general Marcus Agrippa. Both of these aqueducts are still in working order.

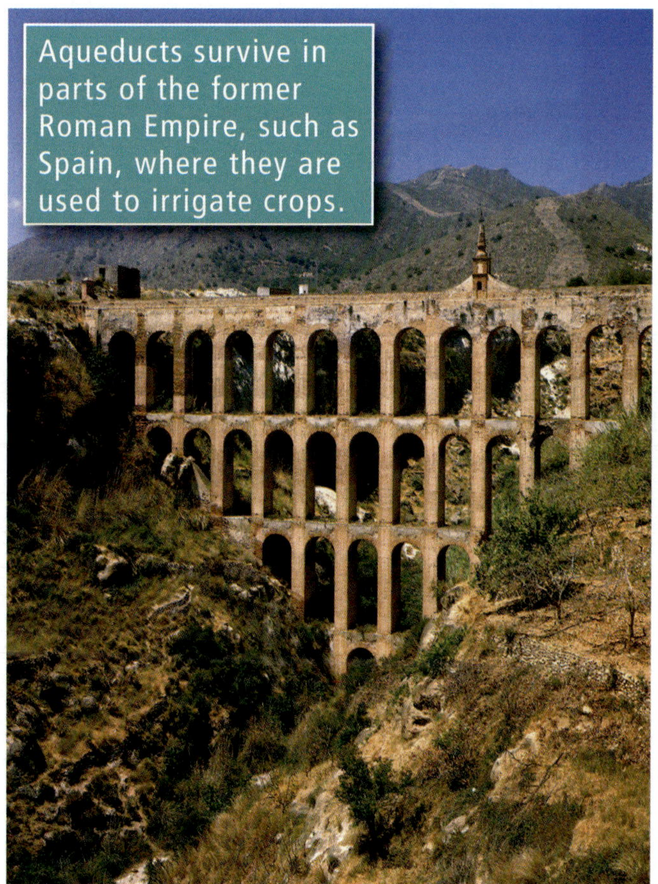

Aqueducts survive in parts of the former Roman Empire, such as Spain, where they are used to irrigate crops.

ACTIVITIES

Transparency

A Roman Road

Examine the diagram and research online to learn more about Roman roads.

1. Describe what the Romans used as a foundation for their roads. How did they make concrete?
2. Many modern roads still follow the route of Roman roads. Investigate where these roads are and when the Romans built the original roads. Which countries have retained Roman roads? Write up your findings.

Weblink

Roman Aqueducts

Watch the video to learn more about Roman aqueducts.

1. What was the gradient of Roman aqueducts? Describe how Roman engineers maintained the water's descent over long distances.
2. Describe the ancient engineering concept that the Romans perfected. How did it revolutionize Roman architecture? Explain the role of the keystone.
3. How many holding tanks in Rome did the water empty into? Infer why the emperor and wealthy Romans having their own water supply is described as a "concept well ahead of its time."

Ancient Artillery

The Greeks invented many of the early artillery weapons, which were later improved by Roman military engineers. The principal artillery devices were catapults. In 399 BC, Dionysius the Elder, ruler of the Greek colony at Syracuse on the island of Sicily, financed a research program to find new weapons for a war with the Carthaginians. His engineers built an arrow-firing catapult that looked like a giant crossbow. They made the bow from strips of wood or horn laminated together in a so-called composite bow. To pull back the bow string, the firing team used a winch that wound back a claw-and-trigger mechanism together with a grooved slider that was held in place by a ratchet. The groove held a 6-foot (2-m) arrow that was fired by moving the trigger to release the claw. The Greeks even made a repeating version of the catapult.

Roman and Greek Catapults

The Romans used a catapult called a ballista. A slightly different Greek catapult design used twisted ropes rather than a bow as the motive power. Two skeins of twisted rope or animal sinew gripped the ends of two short lengths of wood.

One of the earliest weapons used to attack city walls was the slingshot, a handheld catapult.

A drawstring joined the outer ends of these wooden "arms," rather like the bow string of a bow. When the firer winched back the string, the arms twisted the ropes even more. They untwisted with explosive force when the firer pressed a trigger to release the drawstring.

Larger versions of this type of catapult hurled rocks instead of arrows. The Greek mathematician and engineer Archimedes is said to have constructed a catapult capable of throwing a rock weighing 175 pounds (79 kg) a distance of 200 yards (183 m). The huge machine was mounted on a ship for use against the attacking Roman fleet during the siege of Syracuse. Even larger catapults were used on land. In order to stand up to stones weighing up to 350 pounds (159 kg) that were hurled at them, brick city walls had to be built at least 15 feet (4.6 m) thick to withstand an assault by catapults.

Technology Advances

After the decline of the Roman Empire in the late 400s AD, armies in Europe continued to use catapults right through the Middle Ages. They developed the trebuchet, which was a lever system and worked a little like a seesaw. A rock on one end of a pivoted beam was hurled into the air by the action of a larger rock that made the other end of the beam fall. Eventually, all types of catapults were superseded by the introduction of the gunpowder cannon in the fourteenth century.

A Roman Ballista

The Roman name for a catapult was ballista. The Romans adapted the original Greek catapult design to fire 27-inch (69-cm) bolts and often mounted the weapon on a wheeled iron frame. The Roman commander Vespasian used ballistas to great effect in his clashes with Celtic warriors in Britain. Human remains dating from 43 AD that were discovered at the hill fort called Maiden Castle in southern England include a skull drilled through with a ballista-bolt hole. To load the ballista, the slider was pushed forward until the trigger engaged the string. The slider and string were then wound back by the lever to develop tension by bending back the arms. The bolt was put in place and fired by using the trigger to release the string.

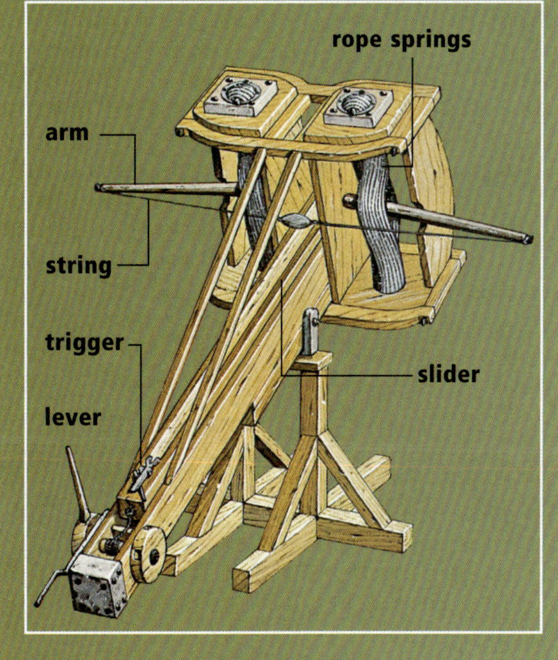

ACTIVITIES

Transparency

A Roman Ballista

Examine the diagram and research online to learn more about Roman ballistas.

1. Where did the Romans get their design for the ballista? What did the bolts measure?
2. Against whom did the Roman emperor Vespasian use ballistas successfully? Describe where evidence has been found that the Romans used ballistas in England.

Weblink

Ancient Roman Artillery

Read the article to learn more about ancient Roman artillery.

1. What was the Roman name for artillery weapons? Describe how these machines worked. Over what distance could they fire their ammunition?
2. Describe the main drawbacks of these machines. Explain where they were mainly used.
3. When did technical manuals for torsion catapults first appear? What inference does the text make about the appearance of technical manuals?

RUBRIC

Researching for a Writing Assignment

Students will complete a thorough research process to prepare for a writing assignment, and organize their research in a logical manner that supports their writing. An exemplary research process will meet the following criteria:

- Creates a goal for the research, based on the topic and working thesis
- Creates specific, thoughtful, and inventive research questions that are relevant to the topic of the writing assignment
- Produces a list of categories, key words, and related ideas to effectively assist in researching
- Uses high-quality sources that pertain to the topic and come in a variety of formats, such as books, journals, primary sources, websites, and databases
- Uses sources that provide balanced research and various perspectives of the topic in question
- Takes notes to highlight the key facts and ideas in order to answer all research questions
- Extracts relevant, detailed information from the sources
- Writes notes in the student's own words
- Organizes the research notes in a clear and concise manner
- Analyzes the information and produces ideas and points to support the working thesis
- Uses an effective and suitable format to present all research
- Properly cites all sources used
- Uses quotations properly and ethically

The observatory in the city of Chichen Itza is aligned to the orbit of the planet Venus, which the Mayans believed was an ally of the god of war.

The Mayan Civilization

The Mayan was the greatest of the early American civilizations. The Maya developed a writing system with about 850 characters. Mayan scholar-priests were skilled astronomers and mathematicians.

The first signs of the emerging Mayan civilization appeared between 300 BC and 100 AD, during the Late Formative Period. During the Classic Period, between 250 and 900 AD, the Maya erected many carved stone pillars, or stelae. Carved pillars record the dates they were made, the names of Mayan nobles, and important events. The Maya also produced books containing **astronomical tables**. Astronomers used observations to discern cycles in astronomical phenomena. They were able to calculate that the Moon completes its cycle 149 times in 4,400 days. The time for one cycle, a lunar month, therefore, was 29.5302 days. The length accepted today is 29.53059 days.

The Maya could predict **solar eclipses**, though not where they would be visible. They were not aware that the Moon orbits Earth and Earth orbits the Sun. This meant that their eclipse dates were based not on orbital calculations but on records. From their records, they deduced that there is never a solar eclipse if the new Moon appears more than 18 days after the day when the Sun crosses the Moon's path.

Mayan astronomers also calculated the average movements of Venus. They achieved an accuracy of one day in 6,000 years. They also realized that Venus is both the morning and evening star.

Numbers

In order to record dates and perform calculations, the Maya needed a number system. In developing the system, Mayan mathematicians introduced two extremely important concepts. These were place values and a symbol for zero, which are both still used in number systems today. A dot represented one, a horizontal dash five, and a picture of a shell represented zero. The Maya were using this notation by about 400 BC. Place values allowed them to write very large numbers clearly and conveniently.

Mayans used the calendar to record specific dates in their history, which they recorded on stone pillars.

The Mayan Calendar

The Mayan calendar was in fact three calendars. The first was based on a sacred year of 260 days arranged in two overlapping cycles, the first comprising the numbers 1 to 13. The second was made up of 20 day names, which were also the names of gods. A number and the name of a god uniquely identified each day in the sacred year, but the sacred calendar was of no use to farmers. For everyday use, there was a calendar based on a solar year. It was divided into 18 months each of 20 days plus five unlucky days, a "period with no name." People believed that someone born at that time was cursed for life.

The third calendar, used for "long counts," consisted of a series of cycles in which 20 kins, or days, made 1 uinal. There were further units of 360 days, 7,200 days, and 144,000 days. The longest cycle was the alautun, of 23,040,000,000 days. For reasons that are not clear, the calendar counted from a zero date on August 13, 3114 BC.

Mayan scholars used supplementary data from a series of astronomical tables containing information about the lunar month and a secondary series based on a formula in order to correct calendar dates. These corrections brought the calendar into line with both the lunar month and solar year. They also had to take account of sacrificial cycles of 4, 9, and 819 days, which were of religious importance.

ACTIVITIES

Video

Breaking the Maya Code #4: The Maya Calendar

Watch the video to learn more about the Maya calendar.

1. Explain what the Maya calendar round is. How long does each cycle last?
2. What was the date that German historian Ernst Förstermann found throughout the Maya world? Explain what conclusion Förstermann came to about this date. Analyze whether his conclusion is reasonable. Might he have reached another conclusion? Give reasons for your answer.

Weblink

Maya Technology

Review the weblink to learn more about Maya technology.

1. Assess why the Maya did not use iron tools. What materials did they make their tools from?
2. Explain why jadeite tools have not been found in royal tombs.
3. What is obsidian? Describe what the Maya used it for.

RUBRIC

Analyzing a Scientific Blog

Students will complete a thorough analysis of a blog that explores scientific events. An exemplary analysis will meet the following criteria:

- Chooses a relevant and meaningful blog
- Provides a working link to the blog
- Identifies the blogger
- Presents information about the blogger
- Assesses the blogger's reliability
- Considers and assesses the blogger's perspective
- Determines the blogger's intended audience
- Determines whether the blogger had first hand knowledge of the topic or event, or whether he or she is reporting as a secondary source
- Summarizes the events that the blogger is covering
- Determines any bias present in the blog postings
- Examines and evaluates any content tags used by the blogger
- Uses additional sources to confirms any claims made by the blog
- Uses correct spelling, grammar, and punctuation

Timeline of Science Discoveries

The prehistoric and classical periods saw many advances in science and technology being made around the world. These are some of the most important breakthroughs. They cover a wide range of fields of science.

	PREHISTORY	7000–5000 BC	5000–3500 BC	3500–2300 BC	2300–1500 BC
Technology	**1,000,000 BC** *Homo erectus* uses hammers made from antlers to create tools. **750,000 BC** Fire is used by *Homo erectus* in France. **30,000 BC** The tally stick is used for counting in Africa and Europe.	**6300 BC** The earliest surviving dugout boat dates from this time. **6000 BC** Clay pottery is produced in Asia Minor. People there also weave cloth and make rope. **6000 BC** The oldest-known pottery in the Americas is produced on the Amazon River.	**5000 BC** Copper is smelted in Egypt and used to make weapons and other implements. **4400 BC** Egyptians weave cloth on a loom, usually linen made from flax. **3500 BC** The wheel is invented in Mesopotamia. It is originally a hand-operated potter's wheel.	**3500 BC** Farmers in Mesopotamia and China use a primitive plow. **3200 BC** The copper–tin alloy bronze is first used in Mesopotamia. **3200 BC** Wheeled vehicles with axles are used in the Middle East. **2800 BC** The Egyptians make papyrus out of crushed reeds.	**2000 BC** Spoked wheels are used on chariots in Egypt and Mesopotamia, and bridles are used on horses. **1950 BC** Farmers in Palestine make plows with iron plowshares. **1500 BC** The Egyptians invent the shadoof for raising water for irrigation.
Sciences	**11,000 BC** Hunter-gatherers in northern Syria cultivate rye. **10,000 BC** Dogs are domesticated in Mesopotamia. **9000 BC** Einkorn wheat is cultivated in Palestine. **8000 BC** In Central America, pumpkins and squashes are domesticated.	**7000 BC** Pigs are domesticated in present-day Turkey. **6500 BC** Rice is grown in China in the delta of the Yangtze River. **6500 BC** Cattle are domesticated in Africa and Asia. **5000 BC** Arable farming begins in Mexico and other parts of Central America.	**5000 BC** Farmers in northern Africa and Ethiopia grow various types of millet as the principal grain crop. **4236 BC** Egyptians introduce a 365-day calendar. **4000 BC** Domestication of horses occurs in Ukraine.	**3400 BC** The Sumerians use picture writing that develops into cuneiform writing. **2950 BC** In China a lunar calendar is developed. **2500 BC** Sumerian traders introduce standard weights. 2500 BC Egyptian physicians begin practicing surgery.	**2300 BC** Astronomers in Babylon study comets and observe the constellations. **1650 BC** Egyptian mathematicians learn how to solve simple equations.

ACTIVITIES

1500–1000 BC	1000–750 BC	750–500 BC	500–250 BC	250 BC–0 AD
1500 BC The Mitanni of western Asia learn how to smelt iron from its ore. **1450 BC** The Egyptians make a water clock that measures time by the rate at which water flows out of the hole. **1100 BC** The Chinese introduce spinning to make yarn from wool and cotton.	**1000 BC** The kite is invented in China, arguably the first heavier-than-air flying object. **900 BC** The Chinese use cast metal coins. **850 BC** The Chinese use natural gas for lighting, using bamboo "pipes." **850 BC** The first known arch bridge built of stone is constructed in Turkey.	**700 BC** Phoenician sailors use biremes, boats with two rows of oars. **515 BC** Philosopher Anaximander of Miletus introduces the sundial to Greece as a means of telling the time. **513 BC** Persian King Darius builds a long pontoon bridge to carry his army across the Bosporus, a narrow stretch of water near Istanbul.	**424 BC** Greek soldiers use a tube of burning charcoal, sulfur, and tar as a flamethrower. **350 BC** Smiths in Greece and Italy begin using coal as a fuel in forges. **250 BC** Greek scientist Archimedes invents the screw pump for raising water for irrigation.	**150 BC** Greeks use a screw press for crushing olives to make olive oil. **80 BC** Vertical waterwheels are introduced in Mediterranean countries for grinding corn. **30 BC** Craftsmen in Syria discover the technique of glassblowing, which the Romans soon adopt.
1361 BC Chinese astronomers record the sighting of a solar eclipse. **1350 BC** An Egyptian text describes the symptoms of the disease leprosy. **1000 BC** The Phoenicians of the Mediterranean develop a 22-letter alphabet.	**950 BC** Farmers in northern and central Europe cultivate oats, better suited than wheat to the region's climate. **900 BC** Farmers in Mesopotamia use irrigation to improve their yields. **763 BC** Babylonian astronomers record a solar eclipse.	**750 BC** Greek poet Homer refers to burning sulfur to fumigate plants and kill pests. **600 BC** The Mayas of Central America make a chocolate drink using cacao. **550 BC** Pythagoras determines the relationship between the length of a vibrating string and the pitch of the note it produces.	**400 BC** Greek physician Hippocrates of Kos describes human anatomy. **330 BC** Greek philosopher Aristotle proposes that Earth is at the center of the Universe and that the Sun, Moon, planets, and stars orbit around it.	**240 BC** Chinese astronomers record what becomes known as Halley's comet. **235 BC** Greek mathematician Eratosthenes of Cyrene calculates the circumference of Earth. **28 BC** Chinese astronomers begin keeping records of sunspots.

Transparency

Timeline of Science Discoveries

Analyze important scientific discoveries from 1,000,000 BC to 28 BC.

1. Why might these discoveries be featured in the timeline? What makes these particular discoveries important?
2. How do you think the people would have viewed these discoveries when they were first revealed? How might their opinions have differed from those of scientists? Why?
3. What effect did these discoveries have on the field of science?
4. How might these discoveries have shaped the world today? What sources can be used to illustrate these effects?

Quiz

1 On what force did all early methods of making fire rely?

2 What were the first crops to be cultivated systematically?

3 How did the spoked wheel benefit Sumerian armies?

4 What is the name of the famous ancient Egyptian picture writing?

5 What does the medical procedure of trepanning involve?

6 For which Egyptian ruler was the first pyramid built?

7 What is the advantage of a lateen sail over normal sails?

8 What was the main food crop of Indo-Aryan farmers on the Ganges Plain?

9 What was the name of the first Roman road, built in 312 BC?

10 How many characters were in the Mayan hieroglyphic writing system?

ANSWERS

1. Friction **2.** Cereals **3.** It made chariots lighter and easier to maneuver. **4.** Hieroglyphics **5.** Cutting a hole in the skull to allow the cause of an illness to escape **6.** Djoser **7.** It allows a ship to be sailed into the wind. **8.** Rice **9.** The Via Appia, Appian Way **10.** About 850

Study the Sources

The history of science is a complicated subject. Historians must be able to understand scientific processes as well as the ways in which history changes because of social, economic, political, or military pressures and opportunities. Adding to the difficulty, the people who recorded advances in the past often did not understand what was actually happening in the scientific developments they were describing.

Consider a major theme discussed in this book. Topics you might choose could be agriculture, metallurgy, engineering, or construction.

Use the internet to find at least two descriptions and at least two images of the topic. Try to find images from China and Arabia as well as European sources. Note how people from different cultures or different centuries portrayed different aspects as being important.

Compare the descriptions and images you find with this book. How accurate do you think the sources are in their scientific descriptions? Do the words or images reflect the science behind what is happening? Why might artists or writers find it difficult to understand what they are looking at?

Key Words

archaeological: related to the study of the past by uncovering and examining the material remains of past societies

artifacts: any objects made by humans

astrologer: a person who studies the stars and planets and their supposed effect on events on Earth

astronomical tables: records designed to enable the calculation of planetary positions, lunar phases, eclipses, and information for calendars

Bronze Age: the period of Asian and European prehistory from about 4000 to 1200 BC, when most tools were made of bronze

domesticated: describes animals or wild plants adapted through selective breeding to make them useful for humans

extinct: no longer existing

flint: an extremely hard type of black quartz found in sedimentary rocks

flywheels: heavy wheels that resist changes in speed and steady the rotation of a shaft

fulcrum: the point on or against which a lever is supported

herbal medicines: medicines made from plants

hieroglyphs: a system of writing that uses pictures to symbolize words

irrigation: the artificial watering of crops to help them grow

lever: a simple machine consisting of a rigid bar pivoted on a fixed point and used to transmit force

lunar: of or relating to the Moon

Mesoamericans: people who lived in what are now the southern part of Mexico and Central America

meteorites: rock fragments of extraterrestrial origin

new Moon: the first visible crescent of the Moon

papyrus: a writing material made by beating together the stems of papyrus reeds

pastoralists: people who primarily live by raising and herding livestock, such as cattle, sheep, and goats

planetarium: an apparatus or display representing the celestial bodies and other astronomical phenomena, and the building or room that contains it

pyramids: structures with a square base and four sloping, triangular sides meeting at the top

rock carving: the depiction of animals, figures, and shapes on a rock surface

solar eclipses: astronomical events in which the Moon blocks all or part of the Sun's light from reaching Earth by passing directly between Earth and the Sun

smiths: people who work with metal

Index

LIGHTBOX

SUPPLEMENTARY RESOURCES

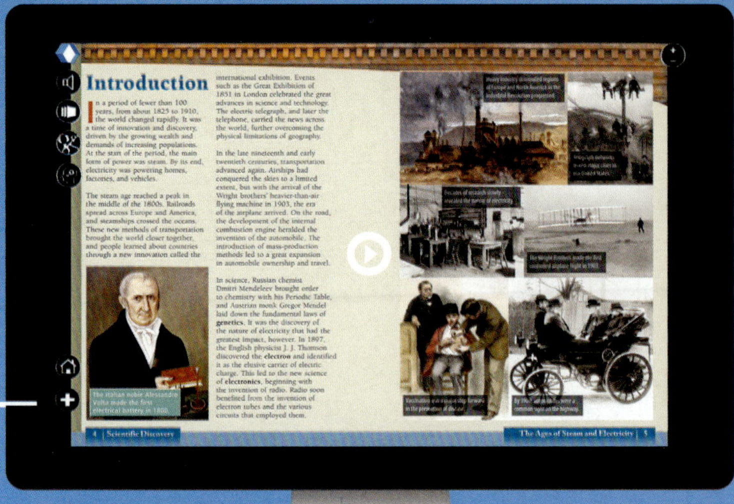

Click on the plus icon found in the bottom left corner of each spread to open additional teacher resources.

- Download and print the book's quizzes and activities
- Access curriculum correlations
- Explore additional web applications that enhance the Lightbox experience

LIGHTBOX DIGITAL TITLES

Packed full of integrated media

VIDEOS

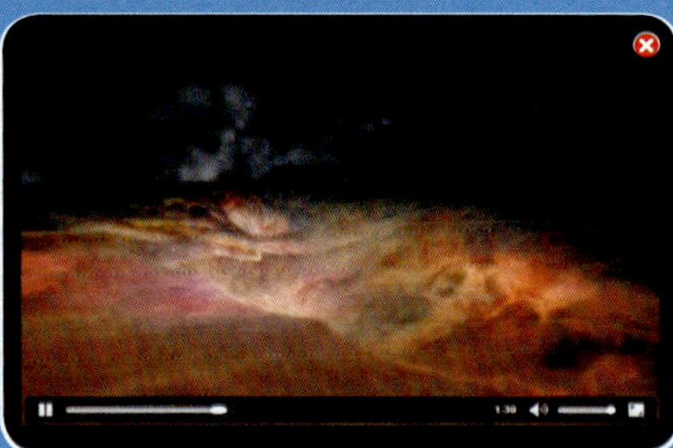

INTERACTIVE MAPS

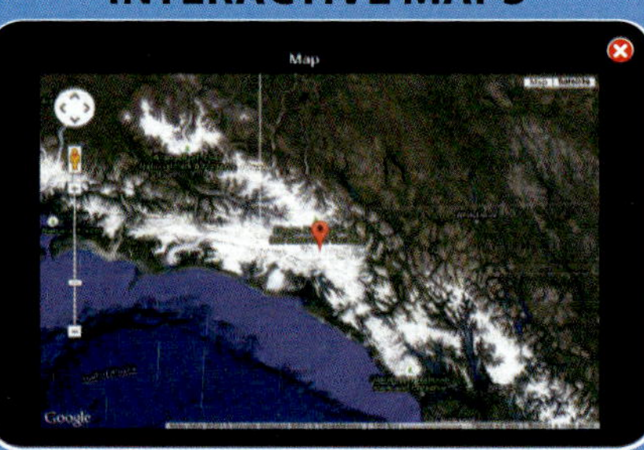

WEBLINKS

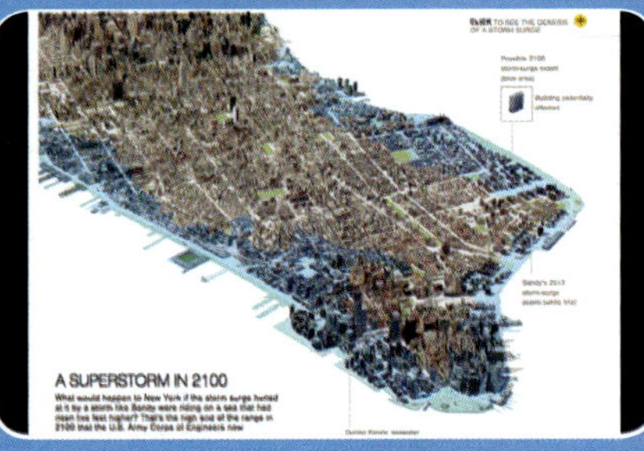

SLIDESHOWS

QUIZZES

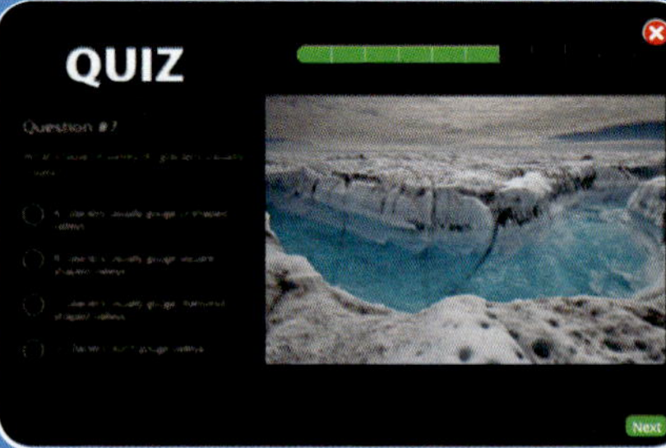

OPTIMIZED FOR

- ✔ TABLETS
- ✔ WHITEBOARDS
- ✔ COMPUTERS
- ✔ AND MUCH MORE!

Published by Smartbook Media Inc.
350 5th Avenue, 59th Floor New York, NY 10118
Website: www.openlightbox.com

First published by Brown Bear Books in 2009

Library of Congress Control Number: 2018941507

ISBN 978-1-5105-3765-1 (hardcover)
ISBN 978-1-5105-3766-8 (multi-user eBook)

Printed in Brainerd, Minnesota, United States
1 2 3 4 5 6 7 8 9 0 22 21 20 19 18

072018
121217

Project Coordinator: Heather Kissock
Art Director: Ana María Vidal

Every reasonable effort has been made to trace ownership and to obtain permission to reprint copyright material. The publisher would be pleased to have any errors or omissions brought to its attention so that they may be corrected in subsequent printings.

The publisher acknowledges Getty Images, Alamy, Newscom, iStock, Shutterstock, and Dreamstime as its primary image suppliers for this title.